The Development of the Trinity

The Evolution of a "New Doctrine"

Glen Davidson, MA

The Development of the Trinity:
The Evolution of a "New Doctrine"

Copyright © 2012
Glen Davidson, MA

ALL RIGHTS RESERVED
No portion of this publication may be reproduced, stored in any electronic system, or transmitted in any form or by any means, electronic, mechanical, photocopy, recording, or otherwise, without written permission from the author. Brief quotations may be used in literary reviews.

All Scripture quotations are from the Authorized King James Version of the Bible unless otherwise noted.

ISBN: 978-07577-4345-0

Printed by:
Pentecostal Publishing House
8855 Dunn Road
Hazelwood, MO 63042

Acknowledgments

I want to thank God for both historical understanding and biblical revelation. I don't have it all down, but what I do see has changed my life. God has been good to me.

First, I want to thank James Smith III, ThD (Harvard University). He is the church history professor at Bethel Seminary and the University of San Diego, as well as a respected historian. I could not have done this research without his guidance and counsel.

Second, I thank God for my wonderful Jewish parents. After our children were grown, my mother, Louisa, completely paid for my seminary education. I could not have researched the subject in this book had it not been for her support.

Finally, my wife, Nancy, is a jewel and deserves utmost recognition. Besides everything else, she endured countless hours of conversation forced on her by my interest in the subject. She has edited the following pages as well. She is a woman "highly to be praised"!

Preface

I rode for two hours on the airplane from Chihuahua to Tijuana with a Bible school student and minister from Ensenada. After going over the clear facts of baptism being performed in the name of Jesus Christ (or similarly stated) in the book of Acts (Acts 2:38; 8:16; 10:48; 19:5; 22:16), we discussed the obvious questions: What about the Godhead? Who is Jesus? Why, when Matthew records that we are to be baptized in the "name of the Father, and of the Son, and of the Holy Ghost," do we find that the apostles baptized in the "name" of Jesus? Was Jesus giving them exact words, or was He "opening their understanding"—that repentance and remission of sins would be in *His* name, beginning at Jerusalem?[1] Why do we find no mention of baptism using the previous formula until about AD 130?

As we landed, my new friend commented, "According to my Christian tradition, this is a new doctrine." I replied, "That is exactly the point." We don't want a new doctrine, but that is exactly what developed in post-apostolic years. The "new doctrine" was that of the trinity.

---

[1] Luke 24:45, 47. We note also that the church did indeed begin at Jerusalem with the outpouring of the Holy Spirit and Peter's opening message (Acts 1:8; 2:4; 2:38). (See also Matthew 16:13-19.)

ORTHODOX ICON OF THE TRINITY

The three persons, according to Gregory of Nyssa,
were like Peter, James, and John.
(Please see pages 79-80.)

Table of Contents

Foreword 1
Introduction 9

After the Apostles of Acts 15
   Clement of Rome 15
   Ignatius 17
   Polycarp 22
   Baptismal Formula 22
   The "Teaching of the Apostles"? 27

Development Part One:
The New Doctrine Is Introduced 29
   The Logos 33
   The Problem in Proverbs 8 36
   Justin Martyr 43

Development Part Two:
The New Doctrine Is Established 47
   Irenaeus 47
   Tertullian 51
   Clement of Alexandria 55
   Origen 57
   Modalism 62
   The Council of Nicea 65
   The Council of Constantinople 70
   The Pre-existence Of Christ 71

    The Cappadocians 75
        Basil of Caesarea 76
        Gregory of Nyssa 78
        Gregory of Nazianzus 80
        Summary of Cappadocians 81

Development Part Three:
The New Doctrine Is Mandated 83
    Augustine 83
    The Athanasian Creed 88
    After the Athanasian Creed 91

The New Doctrine's Terminology:
The Creeds 95
    The Apostles' Creed 96
    The Nicene and
        Nicene-Constantinopolitan Creeds 97
    The Definition of Chalcedon 99
    The Athanasian Creed 100

Non-biblical Words Used in Church History 105

Summary 111

Reflections 117

Annotated Bibliography 127

Foreword

It is impossible to research and write an historical or especially a theological topic without bias. Objectivity is honorable. That has been my intent in this time of study. However, let me begin with a confession so there are no "hidden cards." For more than thirty years I have been part of the Oneness Pentecostal movement. I first fought the doctrine. All I saw was rebaptism in the name of Jesus, and I could not understand its importance.[2] However, things changed. After a season of fasting and prayer, I saw that the "mighty God" was "in Christ, reconciling the world unto himself" (Isaiah 9:6, II Corinthians 5:19). There was such a sweet spirit of revelation! It was not a second person who was kicked out of heaven, but God Himself made the redemption. Jesus was who I had wished He really was.

Now, years have passed, and I have had the opportunity to attend graduate school. I have been privileged to obtain a master's degree in theology from Bethel Seminary with an emphasis in church history. My object of study was the development of the trinity. The booklet you are about to read comes out of this. I entered the study with no axe to

---

[2] E. N. Bell claimed the same problems in his reconciling of the "New Issue" doctrine. However, we'll leave that for another study.

The Development of the Trinity

grind but finished convinced more than ever that we have a message to be proclaimed. The trinity—without any doubt of any historian—was indeed a development. The ideologies that led to and came from this dogma were from the influence of Greek thinking, namely Neo-Platonism.[3]

This theme will be repeated throughout this study: If we just would take the Word of God and church history as they are, we would clearly see that the trinity was something developed as a carnal (human) explanation of revelatory things. Added to that was the extreme problem of the Platonically inspired theory of a second "person"—or deity —in the Godhead that was pre-existent before Jesus' birth. After that came the language of "co-equal," "co-eternal," etc. This crystallized the errors of the church's thinking. The catholic (universal) church had indeed become "Catholic" (as a religion with its own ideas). The new doctrine of the trinity, as Adam Clarke said, pollutes the fount.

Allow me to give you three helps in reading the following pages: First, read the footnotes. Some of them make reference to known historians.[4] When you see their names,

---

[3] Justo González writes, "The long history of a Neoplatonic interpretation of Christianity had made is way into Christian theology through the influence of Justin, Origen, Augustine, . . ." (*The Story of Christianity*, Vol. 2 [Peabody, Ma.: 2001], 51).

[4] Most theologians will recognize names like Jaroslav Pelikan, Otto Heick, Alister McGrath, and Justo González, but not everyone else will be so fortunate. The references, along with the notes about the

Foreword

you may know that the topic is supported by known, respected individuals. This is a main objective of this study. The history facts are just that: facts. Respected, learned historians—most of whom are theologically trinitarian—let us know how the trinity was developed. Other footnotes further discuss a topic. There are times when we hit a "rabbit hole" and go to an interesting topic,[5] but it is best discussed through the footnote rather than the main text.

Second, make sure you don't miss a very informative and exciting section: "Non-biblical words used in church history."[6] Words common to today's Christian culture are "God the Son," "God the Holy Spirit," "Eternal Son," "co-equal," and "co-eternal." However, none of these words were used until many centuries after the first and even second[7] apostles had "finished their courses" and died.

---

authors in the annotated bibliography, will be quite useful in getting acquainted with them. Also, you may take advantage of your own research in this way.

[5] You will find later, for example, that the saying "God in three persons" was likely not popularized until 1861. (I added this as an example of such a footnote!)

[6] Please see the Table of Contents.

[7] Clement of Rome, in his First Epistle to the Corinthians (Ch. 6), mentions that early post-apostolic preachers "finished the course of their faith with steadfastness." He was partially referring to their great trials of faith and persecution, and he acknowledged them as post-apostolic "apostles." We accept his term.

The Development of the Trinity

I realize that non-biblical words do not necessarily indicate error, but it should be obvious that we Christians have accepted words—with their concepts—that are not found in the Scriptures.

Third, make sure you visit the bibliography. You may obtain the books through public libraries and confirm the full intent of historians' remarks. This bibliography is annotated and selected. Many other books were used in this study, but only the most important sources are in this list.

I assume that you have already understood the basics of the Oneness theology before reading this. If not, allow me to briefly review the foundation. The first concept is: God was and is one. He stated this to Israel (Deuteronomy 6:4; 32:39; Isaiah 44:6). The purposely set foundation of monotheism is basic to Scripture and the heart of God.

This should provoke no argument from any reader of the Old Testament. God is called the "Holy One"[8] of Israel. The prophecies of His appearance as God are amazingly enlightening:

Isaiah 40:9: "Say unto the cities of Judah, Behold your God!"

Isaiah 45:22-23: "Look unto me, and be ye saved, all the ends of the earth: for I am God, and there is

---

[8] As William Penn wrote, "He is not the "Holy Three" but the "Holy One." We will leave the details of his writing for the next study!

Foreword

none else. I have sworn by myself, the word is gone out of my mouth in righteousness, and shall not return, That unto me every knee shall bow, every tongue shall swear."

Paul interpreted this "me" that is God as the man Jesus in both Romans 14:11 and Philippians 2:10.

Zechariah 12:10: "They shall look upon me whom they have pierced. . . ."

Malachi 3:1 (NIV): "I will send my messenger, who will prepare the way before me. Then suddenly the Lord you are seeking will come to his temple. . . ."

John the Baptist prepared the way before Jesus, as Mark 1:2-3 tells us.

The mystery of God in Christ in the New Testament is fascinating. He told the Jews, "Before Abraham was, I am" (John 8:58). They tried to stone Him, but He walked away. He said, "I and my Father are one" (John 10:30). In their anger to this, they again tried to stone Him, but He again walked away. Before He was taken to be crucified, He stated, "I am he." They fell backward but immediately afterward apparently did not think about it, for they returned to take him away.

What a glorious mystery! God was manifested as a man. The pre-existence of the "eternal Son of God" is not conducive to monotheism and was a development, as I pray

The Development of the Trinity

you will see in the next pages.

The second concept is this: Acts 2:38 is the hermeneutic key to understanding the rest of the New Testament. In other words, the church began in the Book of Acts. After the power of God filled the lives of the first believers, the visiting crowd asked how they should respond. Peter, who had been given the "keys" to the new kingdom, replied,

> "Repent, and be baptized every one of you in the name of Jesus Christ for the remission of sins, and you shall receive the gift of the Holy Ghost. For the promise is unto you, and to your children, and to all that are afar off, even as many as the Lord our God shall call."

I don't think we (Oneness Pentecostals) have missed it. This was the beginning of the church, and this was the first message. The plan of baptism in water coupled with the baptism of the Holy Ghost was repeated in Acts 8, 10, and 19. No one entered the kingdom in the Book of Acts just by believing. Insistence on water and Spirit has caused the movement to be ostracized by many, but it is still the pattern of the first believers.

There are two more reasons why the movement is often branded as heretical.

First, the Oneness movement appears to some as a revival of modalism (or "modalistic monarchianism").

Foreword

David Bernard denies it,[9] Gregory Boyd confirms it,[10] and some Oneness authors have admitted to some but not all of its similarities.[11] But there is no historical link between modalism and the Oneness revival of the 1900s. So our thinking is not a revival of previous theology, at least not purposely. Our purpose in Oneness is to stay true to the Scriptures, revelatory understanding, God, and our conscience. If that means reworking traditional trinitarian thought, so be it.

Second, we deny that the development of the trinity was spiritually inspired, or "revelatory." The reading of any history on the subject, though, will confirm that our analysis is correct. My own hunger for historical facts caused long hours of research that far exceeded any requirement of graduate school. This book is the "tip of the iceberg" of a

---

[9] David Bernard is indisputably the most prolific writer in defense of Oneness Pentecostalism. He admits that there are similarities but is cautious of making full theological connections.

[10] Gregory Boyd is well known for his criticism of Oneness Pentecostalism. He is a "defector" from the movement. His book, *Oneness Pentecostals and the Trinity*, relates his theology and biography.

[11] Talmadge French, for example, calls the beginnings of the Oneness movement "simultaneous" rather than "chronological" modalism in his historical book, *Our God is One: The Story of Oneness Pentecostals* (Indianapolis: Voice & Vision Publications, 1999), 15.

The Development of the Trinity

mound of information. I could not find even one historian who concluded that the trinity was the result of revelation. The overwhelming consensus was that the dogma was developed by the minds of men.[12] There are many, many quotes that might make the reading of this booklet a bit laborious, but please understand their purpose: This study is not to be filled with my own opinion but the opinions of scholar-historians far better than myself. My hopes and prayers are for your personal understanding to be increased. I pray this study will help, bless, and enlighten you.

---

[12] Some ministers, not scholars, have said that the Holy Spirit must have gradually inspired the patristic church leaders. But, again, no historian has that opinion.

Introduction

After Jesus rose from the dead, He promised to fill the first church with the Holy Spirit. This beginning of the New Testament church was explosive. The first believers experienced a dynamic transformation, changing their cowardice to boldness. Immediately after the Day of Pentecost, a lame man, born as such and then over forty years old, was healed at the front doors of the Temple. Fire from heaven "consumed the sacrifice" (II Chronicles 7:1) of the waiting disciples. The spiritual undercurrent was deep, vigorous, and "violent" (Matthew 11:12). Two events were the focus of these fortunate people. First, Jesus had risen from the dead. Second, God's power was in full operation.

In this light one scholar writes: "for about a century after the close of the New Testament period—or, until about the end of the second century, there is no new and striking development of Christological opinion with the Church."[13]

When we read of developments later in church history, we cannot help but see a decline in focus and in power. The introduction to Philip Schaff's famed *Early Church Fathers* reads:

---

[13] Alan Richardson, *Creeds in the Making: A Short Introduction to the History of Christian Doctrine* (Great Britain, Macmillan Company, 1935), 31-32.

The Development of the Trinity

Disappointment may be the first emotion of the student who comes down from the mount where he has dwelt in the tabernacles of evangelists and apostles: for these disciples are confessedly inferior to the masters; they speak with the voices of infirm and fallible men, and not like the New Testament writers, with the fiery tongues of the Holy Ghost.[14]

In terms of power, the first church was vibrant. In general doctrine, the believers were monotheistic. The first responders were Jewish leaders who had arrived at Jerusalem for the fulfillment of celebration of the "feast of weeks," or Pentecost (Deuteronomy 16:16). According to one historian, they were prone to "regard their monotheism as a badge of their nationality and as a principal difference between their own religion and that of their heathen neighbors."[15] The early church, in David Wright's words, was "distinguished from paganism by its unqualified monotheism."[16] Their "doctrine of one God," according to

---

[14] A. Cleveland Coxe, Introduction, *Early Church Fathers: The Translations of The Writings of the Fathers down to AD 325*, ed. Philip Schaff, [CD-ROM] (Waco, Texas: Epiphany Software, 2006).

[15] Richardson, 34.

[16] David Wright, "Trinity," *Encyclopedia of Early Christianity*, ed. Everett Ferguson (New York: Garland Publishers, 1997), 1142. Wright is the Professor Emeritus of Patristic and Reformed Christianity

Introduction

J.N.D. Kelly, "formed the background and indisputable premises of the church's faith. . . . It was her bulwark against pagan polytheism."[17]

But now we have an added feature to monotheism. Jesus Christ was a man, but was He more? Was He God? As Jaroslav Pelikan asks, "Is the divine that has appeared on earth and reunited man with God identical with the supreme divine, which rules heaven and earth, or is it a demigod?"[18] How would the church deal with these questions?

Later Pelikan continues, "The dogma of the Trinity was developed as the church's response to a question about the identity of Jesus Christ. Was he, or was he not, equal in his divine existence with the Creator and Lord of heaven and earth?"[19] David Wright represents a common view of what took place in answering the question:

> The doctrine of the Trinity is one of the most distinctive and fundamental tents of the Christian faith. . . . It was during the patristic centuries that

---

at the University Of Edinburgh.

[17] J.N.D. Kelly, *Early Christian Doctrines* (London: Adam and Charles Black, 1958), 87.

[18] Jaroslav Pelikan, *The Christian Tradition; A History of the Development of Doctrine, Vol. I: The Emergency of the Catholic Tradition (100-600)* (Chicago: University of Chicago Press, 1971), 172.

[19] Ibid., 226.

The Development of the Trinity

the church's Trinitarian faith assumed the shape it has largely retained throughout its history.[20]

If the trinity became fundamental to Christian faith, we should examine its teaching. The word "trinity" is neither mentioned as a word nor consciously spelled out in the Scriptures.[21] It is clear that this system of belief was a development. This is the point that should be noted by any Bible student or minister. Alister McGrath, a well-known

---

[20] Wright, Ibid.

[21] Two verses are often used as proof texts by trinitarians: Matthew 28:19 and II Corinthians 13:14. Matthew 28:19 was not a proclamation of three deities but an announcement of the resurrection of Christ and Jesus' great commission to the apostles. If a trinitarian theological statement were meant to be given, it would be noticed in Jesus' words. But Jesus said, "All power is given unto me"; and "I am with you alway" not "they. . . ." Further, the parallel account of Luke 24:45, 47 shows that Jesus was opening "their understanding" that forgiveness of sins would be preached in "his name," beginning at Jerusalem. The fulfilling event was recorded in Acts 2, when Peter preached baptism "in the name of Jesus Christ" (Acts 2:38).

The other reference, II Corinthians 13:14, was the end of Paul's (most likely fourth) letter to the Corinthians. The genre is a benediction, not a doctrinal statement. Paul was closing his letters but not trying to instruct the church on matters of relationships within the divine triad.

Introduction

writer for seminaries, states that "the mind of the church thus developed gradually." He neatly and correctly puts the historical maturity of the trinity into three stages:

1. The recognition of the full divinity of Jesus Christ.
2. Divinity of the Spirit.
3. The definitive formulation of the doctrine of the Trinity . . . determining their mutual relationship.[22]

The first stage is biblical. The "same substance" theology was established, as we shall see, in the first council of Nicea. The second stage took place before and during the council of Constantinople. By then, the view had become became philosophical and extra-biblical. The Holy Spirit had not yet been defined as a "person" until this era but now was joining the other two. By the third stage, the word "persons" meant more than was originally intended, and all three "people" in the Godhead could talk with and love each other. The word "trinity" from the 200s now had taken on new definitions. The study of the development of this "trinity" concept will be the subject of the following pages.

---

[22] Alister McGrath, *The Christian Theology Reader. Second Edition* (Malden, Ma.: Blackwell Publishing, 2001), 184-185.

After the Apostles of Acts

The first stage of the apostles is, of course, recorded for us in the Book of Acts. The development of the trinity did not seriously begin until about AD 130. Before we begin this study, though, we will briefly look at the era after the first apostles. The "post-apostolic" age in this era included Clement of Rome, Ignatius of Antioch, and Polycarp of Smyrna. Historians, for the most part, note the particular theological tone of these writers as being "modalistic" (a belief system very similar to modern Oneness Pentecostalism).

In spite of the well known "monarchian" language of these preachers, some trinitarians still note that the writings from this era may indeed may have pre-trinitarian hints, though they lack the substance of its definition. We will attempt to address these claims.

Clement of Rome (d. AD 101)

This preacher continually exalted Christ as "his God." Since his years are so close to the age of the apostles, this is noteworthy. (Most historians believe him to be the same Clement to whom Paul referred in Philippians 4:3.) Clement's famous Epistle to the Corinthians is very close to New Testament language.

Are there objections to this view of Clement? Yes, as just discussed, some trinitarian historical theologians have claimed that there seem to be indicative hints of future trinitarianism in chapters 46 and 58. Chapter 46 reads:

> Have we not (all) one God and one Christ? Is there not one Spirit of grace poured out upon us? And have we not one calling in Christ? Why do we divide and tear to pieces the members of Christ, and raise up strife against our own body, and have reached such a height of madness as to forget that "we are members one of another"? Remember the words of our Lord Jesus Christ, how He said, "Woe to that man (by whom offences come)!"[23]

The language is also very reminiscent of many of excerpts of Paul. This cannot be true trinitarianism but a reflection of the Scriptures. This particular passage could be an allusion to Paul's letter to the Ephesians (4:4-6).[24] The other cry of future trinitarianism comes from Chapter 58:

> For, as God liveth, and as the Lord Jesus Christ and the Holy Ghost live,—both the faith and hope of the elect, he who in lowliness of mind, with instant gentleness, and without repentance hath

---

[23] This and other writings are found in Schaff, *Early Church Fathers*.

[24] This is also the opinion expressed by David Bernard, *Oneness and Trinity, AD 100-300: The Doctrine of God in Ancient Writing* (Hazelwood, Mo.: Word Aflame Press, 1991), 31.

After the Apostles of Acts

observed the ordinances and appointments given by God—the same shall obtain a place and name in the number of those who are being saved through Jesus Christ, through whom is glory to Him for ever and ever. Amen.[25]

Gregory Boyd, in typical support of trinitarianism, writes that this passage "presupposes the commonality of Trinitarian language in his day...."[26] That would be a valid statement but for the problem of interpolation. It was commonly practiced in the Middle Ages. The words above were from the 1056 copy (used by Schaff).[27] The older copy of this, however, does not have these words in it. We may safely assume Clement did not use trinitarian vocabulary.

In a general historical view, we know the trinitarian doctrine had not developed profoundly enough to popularly employ the above language. In fact, this interpolation indicates an attempt in later ages to justify the trinity!

Ignatius (AD 35–107)

Ignatius, most likely a disciple of John,[28] has been

---

[25] Schaff, *Early Church Fathers*.

[26] Gregory Boyd, *Oneness Pentecostals and the Trinity* (Grand Rapids: Baker Books, 1992), 149.

[27] See Bernard, ibid.

[28] Coxe, ibid., and Bernard, *Oneness and Trinity*, 32. Most think that both Ignatius and Polycarp

The Development of the Trinity

well documented.[29] He is even more known for his "Oneness"—or God in Christ—statements: "For our God Jesus Christ was conceived by Mary according to God's plan."[30] In Christ we see "existing in flesh; true life in death; both of Mary and of God."[31] "For our God, Jesus Christ, was, according to the appointment of God, conceived in the womb by Mary, of the seed of David."[32] "Permit me to be an imitator of the passion of Christ, my God."[33] "I glorify

---

were disciples of John. If this is so, it is significant. Both men used "Oneness" language emphatically.

[29] Ignatius is known for his seven letters (perhaps thirteen) to the churches. We have short versions, medium versions, and long versions. It is obvious that the later versions were the ones that were changed in accordance to the later theologies of the trinity. For example: "Farewell in God the Father, and in Jesus Christ our common hope" (Epistle to the Ephesians, Ch. 21) turns into: "Fare ye well in God the Father, and the Lord Jesus Christ, our common hope, and in the Holy Ghost." Scholars such as J. B. Lightfoot (*The Apostolic Fathers*) agree that interpolations are "anachronistic"—they clearly belong to an age when the trinity was more developed.

[30] Kelly, *Doctrines*, 92.

[31] Ignatius, Epistle to the Ephesians, Ch 7.

[32] Ibid., Ch. 18.

[33] Ignatius, Epistle to the Romans, Ch. 6.

After the Apostles of Acts

God, even Jesus Christ."[34] He often refers to Christ Jesus as "our God, God incarnate, and God manifest as man."[35] In summary of his theology, Pelican writes that Ignatius "praised the Invisible, who for our sake became visible, the Impassible, who became subject to suffering on our account and for our sake endured everything."[36] Another historian writes that when Ignatius "speaks of an outcoming of Christ from God, he means the Incarnation, and not anything previous."[37] Ignatius' emphasis of God in Christ was so vigorous that "many historians have called him modalistic."[38]

Ignatius believed that incarnation produced God in the form of man. He clearly defended what would later be called modalism: He told his generation to

> "neither introduce a multiplicity of gods, nor yet deny Christ under the pretence of (maintaining) the unity of God. . . . Whosoever, therefore, declares that there is but one God, only so as to take away the divinity of Christ, is a devil, and an

---

[34] Ignatius, Epistle to the Smyrneans, Ch. 1.

[35] Ibid.

[36] Pelikan, 177.

[37] Henry Pace, William Percy; *Dictionary of Christian Biography.*

[38] Bernard, *Oneness and Trinity*, 32. I realize this comment is from a Oneness writer, but I include this because of its supporting arguments.

The Development of the Trinity

enemy of all righteousness."[39]

Ignatius was not alone. This was the climate of the age. The noted historian Pelikan writes:

> Such praises as "God is born", the "suffering God", or "the dead God" had so established themselves in the unreflecting usage of Christians that even Tertullian, for all his hostility to the Monarchies, would not avoid speaking this way.[40]

Even further, Pelikan writes in strong words. First, he says:

> The oldest surviving sermon[41] of the Christian church opened with the words:
> "Brethren, we ought so to think of Jesus Christ as of God, as of the judge of living and dead. And we ought not to belittle our salvation; for when we belittle him, we expect also to receive little."

Then he goes on to say that

> Clearly it was the message of what the church be-

---

[39] Ignatius, Epistle to the Antiochenes, Chapters 1, 5.

[40] Pelikan, ibid.

[41] Pelikan is referring to the Second Epistle of Clement (of Rome).

lieved and taught that "God" was an appropriate name for Jesus Christ.[42]

Ignatius held strong also to the humanity of Christ.[43] We have no problem with that. In the case of Ignatius, we understand that he was battling the contemporary problem of Docetism.[44] An interesting remark regarding this comes from Pelikan: "Yet the very existence of Docetism is also a testimony to the tenacity of the conviction that Christ had to be God, even at the cost of his true humanity."[45] Pelikan, as noted in the bibliography, is one of the foremost respected theological historians who are relied upon today. Are there objections? Yes, some of Ignatius's greetings in the letters were "interpolated" with expressions such as "God the Father and the Son Jesus Christ and the Holy Spirit." Historians are in agreement that these are indeed additions.[46]

In summary, the theologies of both Clement and

---

[42] Pelikan, 173.

[43] González, 80.

[44] Ibid. Docetism was the belief that Jesus' physical body was an illusion, as was His crucifixion; that is, Jesus only seemed to have a physical body and to physically die.

[45] Pelikan, 174.

[46] Jim Smith, ThD (Harvard University), who supervised this study, wrote his doctoral thesis on this subject. More information may be supported, but the fact of interpolation is the common agreement.

The Development of the Trinity

Ignatius was clearly what would be termed as "modalistic." A second pre-existent God did not walk Galilee's shores. The Incarnation was clearly God manifested in the flesh.[47]

Polycarp (AD 65–155)

Polycarp is often thought of as the next apostle after John. Polycarp was actually born after Ignatius. We do not have much literature preserved from him. We do note, though, that his famous words at his martyrdom were: "Eighty-six years I have served Christ, and He never did me any wrong. How can I blaspheme my King who saved me?" He was "Christocentric" in his thinking.

Baptismal Formula

The notice of the formula of words accompanying baptism is enlightening. It is evident that baptism in the name of Jesus Christ (or a similar expression), which was

---

[47] William Chalfant, unpublished comments. He was kind enough to review this manuscript and make some remarks. He comments here: "For the trinitarian, the Incarnation had to produce a second divine person and not God the Father Himself. They then retrofitted their concept of a second divine person into their concept of God of at first two divine persons and then later three divine persons, coming up with such imaginations as 'eternally begotten,' as we will see later in Origen."

to have begun "at Jerusalem" (Luke 24:47), did indeed begin in that city in Acts 2. This formula was repeated in Samaria (Acts 8:16), was "commanded" by Peter at Caesarea (Acts 10:48), and was again used by Paul in Ephesus (Acts 19:5). Paul himself, upon his conversion, was told by Ananias to be baptized, "calling on the name of the Lord" —the Lord he had just met. Not one example is given in the first church's history of Acts that repeats the trinitarian words of Matthew 28:19 verbatim.

Baptism in the name of Jesus was not only the pattern of the first church (Acts 2:38; 8:12; 10:48; 19:5, 22:16) but was the fulfilling of Matthew 28:19. Whereas Matthew recorded that the apostles were to baptize in the "name of the Father, and of the Son, and of the Holy Ghost," Luke wrote in a parallel passage (Luke 24:45-47, NIV) that Jesus "opened their minds so they could understand the Scriptures" and thus "repentance and forgiveness of sins [would] be preached in his name . . . , beginning at Jerusalem."

Important to the understanding of text is its genre and setting. In the case of Matthew 28, Jesus was giving the great commission's mandate to baptize and to teach. Once again, we note this: He was also opening their understanding to His deity and mission as the Messiah. He was surely not attempting to promote a doctrine of a divine trinity consisting of co-equal, co-eternal persons. Jesus said, "I" will be with you, not "they."

We cannot find even one example of the "name of the Father, and of the Son, and of the Holy Ghost" in the Book of Acts. After the Book of Acts, we turn to church history. Heick writes that "at first baptism was administered

The Development of the Trinity

in the name of Jesus, but gradually in the name of the Triune God: Father, Son and Holy Spirit."[48] Why did the baptismal formula change? He gives his explanation:

> Since the earliest Christians were Jews who already believed in the one God, it was not necessary for them to reaffirm that faith. The essential thing for them was to confess their faith in Jesus Christ, hence the use of the older Christological form. . . . This change from the Christological to the Trinitarian form was to be expected when the Gentiles were coming into the Church.[49]

Other trinitarians have used this logic, including Cyprian in the third century. The explanation is problematic, however. The new converts of Cornelius's house at Caesarea were not Jews, but notably Gentiles (Acts 10). Still, Peter "ordered that they be baptized in the name of Jesus Christ" (Acts 10:48, NIV; KJV says "commanded"). According to Heick, the changes began to occur about AD 130 to 140.[50] Many other documents give support to the change of baptism around this time.[51] Again, for at least one

---

[48] Otto Heick, *A History of Christian Thought,* Vol. I (Philadelphia: Fortress Press, 1965), 53.

[49] Heick, 87.

[50] Ibid.

[51] Word Aflame Press (Tract #1567226140) of United Pentecostal Church quotes *Encyclopedia of*

After the Apostles of Acts

hundred years after Jesus' resurrection, the words "in the name of the Father, and of the Son, and of the Holy Ghost" were not found in the baptismal formula but rather the "name of Jesus Christ" or similarly used words.

The issue of baptism may seem light at first; nevertheless, it was the pivotal point where the trinity took its root.[52] Even today we can read modern ministers who have been influenced by the developed use of Matthew 28:19. One preacher announces that: "Baptism by water in the

---

Religion and Ethics (1951), II, 384, 389; *Interpreter's Dictionary of the Bible* (1962), 1, 351; *Hastings' Dictionary of the Bible* (1898), I, 241; Williston Walker, *A History of the Christian Church* (1947), 58; *The New Schaff-Herzog Encyclopedia of Religious Knowledge* (1957), I, 435; *Canney's Encyclopedia of Religions* (1970), 53; and *Encyclopedia Britannica*, 11th ed. (1910), II, 365. All these are in agreement with Heick's above remark.

[52] The issue of baptism was alive in the fourth century. The document, "A Treatise on Rebaptism by an Anonymous Writer" speaks of baptism "in the name of Jesus Christ our Lord." (See Schaff, *Early Church Fathers*.) The main controversy in this paper was over baptism of those who had left the (general) church and then returned. Still, the controversy of Matthew 28:19 versus Acts 2:38 is touched upon, supporting the name of Jesus. As the issue of the trinity developed, many such as Tertullian and Augustine referred specifically to Matthew 28:19 to support their views.

The Development of the Trinity

name of the Trinity has been practiced by the church from its beginning."[53] Another concurs, writing: "The form of baptism, therefore, has been always understood as an irrefutable argument for the doctrine of the Trinity, or that the Son and Holy Spirit are equal with the Father."[54]

History cannot support these statements, nor can the Word of God. Jesus was enlightening their understanding to His deity, not explaining three co-equal, co-eternal persons. Some through the ages have been honest with such trinitarian explanations. Dwight L. Moody, reflecting on what he was taught about the persons' distinctions, said:

> If you ask do I understand what is thus revealed in Scripture, I say "no." But my faith bows down before the inspired Word and I unhesitatingly believe the great things of God when even reason is blinded and the intellect confused.[55]

What sort of faith is this? It is a "trusting" faith but not a revelatory faith. The trust is in the so-called "Church Fathers." It is a faith that hides in the works of the post-apostolic trinitarian composers but not in the word of God or in the illumination of truth.

---

[53] J. Vernon McGee in his commentary on Matthew 28:19.

[54] Albert Barnes, *Notes on the New Testament*, commentary on the above verse.

[55] Dwight L. Moody, *Secret Power*.

After the Apostles of Acts

The "Teaching of the Apostles"?

So far we have touched upon three well-known preachers after Acts. Also, we have seen that the baptismal formula changed. Scholars and historians have supported the correct historicity of baptism changing to the trinitarian formula in the second century. If there has been a debate over this at all, it has been over a document the *Didache*, or "The Teaching." The manuscript has also been called "The Teaching of the Apostles," intimating that the writings were actually authorized by the first apostles. The *Didache* states that converts were to be baptized "in running water in the name of the Father and of the Son and of the Holy Spirit."[56] This of course is trinitarian and is supposedly in the days of the apostles. However, it is important to mention the two reasons why we cannot consider it.

First, most scholars today do not place the date of this document until well after the first century.[57] Further,

---

[56] Kelly, *Creeds*, 66. Two chapters later, however, the unknown author speaks of these same converts as "those who have been baptized in the name of the Lord." We are dealing, though, with the first quote from the *Didache*.

[57] Millard Erickson, for example, mentions that the *Didache* was written in the second century. His facts are considered correct by most seminaries. (Millard Erickson, *Contemporary Options in Eschaology*, Grand Rapids: Baker Book House, 1982: 128.) Jim Smith, a respected historian (Professor at the

The Development of the Trinity

according to the *Encyclopedia of Religion and Ethics*, scholars generally date the first mention of the threefold formula not to the *Didache*, but to Justin,[58] which would place the "The Teachings" after Justin, sometime at least in the second century. Second, it was common practice by the second century to interpolate the supposed writings to fit into theologies or beliefs that were forming. The prominent historian J.N.D. Kelly writes that the words were "borne out of the church's practice in regard to the formulary in succeeding generations."[59]

Again, for two reasons we cannot use the *Didache*: First, the dates are not truly in the days of the apostles. Second, it appears that the words were interpolated by those who would predate trinitarianism. The doctrine of the trinity would not develop until years after the apostles and after the dates when the *Didache* was written.

University of San Diego and Bethel University, editor of Christian History, etc.), concurs with him.

[58] Kirsopp Lake, "Baptism, Early Christian," *Encyclopedia of Religion and Ethics*, 2:389 (Quoted by Bernard, *Oneness and Trinity*, 53).

[59] Ibid., 42.

Development Part One: The New Doctrine Is Introduced

We are finally getting to the subject. In the age of the Greek Apologists (AD 130–180), we find the new doctrine beginning to formulate. To fully understand this era, we must understand somewhat the underlying Greek philosophies that the Christian culture had to battle. Socrates, Plato, and Aristotle (and Philo as Jesus' contemporary[60]) had laid a foundation that was definitive not only of God but also of the creative properties of deity. The Greek idea of God was one of being "transcendent" and "impassible."[61] The Greeks felt that the supreme Being was "too lofty and holy to have communications with this world."[62] Richardson comments that "such a view of God strikes at the root of the Christian doctrine of Incarnation by denying the possibility of divine condescension."[63] Olson and English describe the Greek view of God's impassibility as *apthathei*—without emotion. They note that this feature

---

[60] Richardson, 42. "Philo taught in Alexandria his doctrine of the Logos while Jesus worked in the carpenter's shop at Nazareth."

[61] Ibid., 36.

[62] Ibid.

[63] Richardson, 37.

The Development of the Trinity

is "essential to the nature of God" in first-century Greek thinking.[64]

It was to this philosophy that the Christians found the need to respond "apologetically"—making sense to the contemporary culture. Richardson says "the pagan idea of God as utterly impassible and transcendent made its presence felt among those who called themselves Christians."[65] Adolf Harnack writes:

> The Gospel was Hellenized in the second century in so far as the Gnostics in various ways transformed it into a Hellenistic religion for the educated. The Apologists (argued that) Christianity was the realization of an absolutely moral theism. This transformation of religion into a philosophic system would not have been possible had not Greek philosophy itself happened to be in the process of development into a religion.[66]

He continues later to say that the Christian response to Greek thinking was "a marvelous attempt to present Chris-

---

[64] Roger Olson and Adam English, *Pocket History of Theology* (Downers Grove, Ill.: InterVarsity Press, 2005), 29.

[65] Richardson, 61.

[66] Adolph Harnack, *History of Dogma,* Vol. III, trans. Neil Buchanan (New York: Dover Publications, 1961), 174-175.

tianity to the world as a religion which is the true philosophy, and as the philosophy of the true religion."[67]

Otto Heick concurs:

> The theology of the Apologists is philosophical in form.... The method, however, becomes dangerous. In the course of time language will inevitably affect the content of its message. In this respect the Apologists set a bad example for succeeding generations.[68]

Heick is right.

Also agreeing with this is Justo González:

> The concept of God which the apologists took from Hellenistic philosophy and which emphasized the divine immutability would long be a burden on Christian theology.[69]

Vergilus Ferm, PhD, head of the Department of Philosophy, Wooster College, writes that the "Apologists represented, on the whole, non-Jewish Christian converts trained to think in Hellenistic terms."[70]

---

[67] Harnack, 177.

[68] Heick, 6.

[69] González, 122.

[70] Vergilius Ferm, *A History of Philosophical Systems* (New York: The Philosophical Library,

The Development of the Trinity

Louis Berkhof also makes observations of the era's Christian philosophers:

> It must be admitted that they represented Christianity largely in terms of philosophy, that they did not clearly discriminate between philosophy and theology, and their representation of the truths of revelation, and particularly of the Logos doctrine, suffered from an admixture of Greek philosophical thought.[71]

We have quoted from several respected historians. It should be highlighted in our minds: The development of the trinitarian thought was undisputedly, undoubtedly rooted in Greek thinking. Yet blatantly ignored was Paul's warning to the church in Colossians. Because of the importance of this, we will look at two versions of this passage.

> Beware lest any man spoil you through philosophy and vain deceit, after the tradition of men, after the rudiments of the world, and not after Christ. For in him dwelleth all the fulness of the Godhead bodily (Colossians 2:8-9, KJV).

1950), 145.

[71] Louis Berkhof, *The History of Christian Doctrines* (Carlisle, Penn.: The Banner of Truth, 1937), 60.

Part One: The New Doctrine Is Introduced

See to it that no one takes you captive through hollow and deceptive philosophy, which depends on human tradition and the basic principles of this world rather than on Christ. For in Christ all the fullness of the Deity lives in bodily form (NIV).

Paul was notably cautious of philosophy. Living in the Greco-Roman world, he not only knew of the dangers of carnal thinking, but it appears he prophesied of the dangers of a coming age when the revelation of God in Christ would be polluted. We now go to the main part of the problem.

The Logos

The word *Logos* was indeed biblical, in particular in the first chapter of the Gospel of John. Logos was with God yet was God. It is similar to our spoken word. If one speaks his "word," it is a part of him. The word may be isolated but only for its view of function; it is not separated from the individual. The Greek Apologists[72] believed differently. First, God was not capable of emotion and interaction. Therefore, He had created the Logos that was separate from Him. This Logos was actually pre-existent to Bethlehem's incarnation. We will see they identified the Logos as the pre-existent Son of God. Because of the importance of this development, we first offer the writings of five well-respected historians:

---

[72] As we stated, this included Philo, a contemporary of Jesus (Bernard, *Oneness and Trinity*, 64).

The Development of the Trinity

The Apologists did not have the biblical conception of the Logos, but somewhat resembling that of Philo. . . . God generated the Logos out of His own being and thus gave Him personal existence. . . . It would be noted particularly that the Logos of the Apologists, in distinction from the philosophical Logos, had an independent personality.[73]

The Apologists taught that it was through the Logos that God created the world. God, being spaceless and infinite, was in need of the Logos as a middle being to bridge the gap and chasm between him and the world.[74]

Stoicism was the philosophical system that most influenced the development of Christian thought. Its doctrine of the Logos, its elevated moral tone, and its doctrine of natural law made a profound impression on Christian thinking.[75]

In discussing the relation of the Son to the Father, the Apologists introduced the term "Logos" from John's Gospel. This was attended, however, with

---

[73] Berkhof, 58. Thus we see the roots of the problem. Berkhof writes that the Logos is independent. How "independent" is your word from yourself?

[74] Heick, 59.

[75] González, 50.

Part One: The New Doctrine Is Introduced

the danger of identifying John's Logos with that of Philo.[76]

The Logos appeared as the angel of the covenant, and in the fullness of time he took upon himself our nature. Although Christ and the Logos were identified, the historical Christ was pushed into the background, and the Son of God was understood to be the pre-existent Logos.[77]

Here is the crux of the problem. The Logos was then linked to the Son. Thus the Son was pre-existent. Loofs writes:

The transfer of the concept "Son" to the preexistent Christ is the most significant factor in the pluralistic distortion of the Christian doctrine of God. . . . The development of doctrine [now included] the divine doctrine of Sonship grounded in preexistence.[78]

It is amazing that trinitarian writers admit to this part of the historical development. Yet historians see the problems inherent in the trinitarian development. Well-respected

---

[76] Heick, 45. Not only was John 1 used, but Proverbs 8 as well. We will have more on this later.

[77] Heick, 61.

[78] Loofs, *Nestoriana: Die Fragmente des Destorius*. (Halle, 1905), 314-315. Quoted by Pelikan, 189.

The Development of the Trinity

historian Berkhof writes, "The Logos doctrine of the Apologetes (sic) . . . did not give general satisfaction. . . . The doctrine of the Logos as a separate divine Person appeared to endanger the unity of God, or monotheism."[79] I appreciate his honesty!

Most current ministers are unaware that the doctrine of pre-existent sonship was even developed. Many accept it as Bible doctrine without understanding its implications and challenges to biblical monotheism.

The Problem in Proverbs 8

Amazingly, there have been many former (Justin, Tertullian, and Augustine, for example) and present-day theologians who have grossly misinterpreted the "wisdom" of Proverbs 8. They have claimed that the Logos became Christ sometime before the incarnation at Bethlehem, and this is supposedly proven by Proverbs 8:22-31. This has been an enormous problem. We will therefore pause here to first examine the Scripture:

> The LORD possessed me in the beginning of his way, before his works of old. I was set up from everlasting, from the beginning, or ever the earth was. When there were no depths, I was brought forth; when there were no fountains abounding with water. Before the mountains were settled, before the hills was I brought forth: while as yet he

---

[79] Berkhof, 77.

Part One: The New Doctrine Is Introduced

had not made the earth, nor the fields, nor the highest part of the dust of the world. When he prepared the heavens, I was there: when he set a compass upon the face of the depth: when he established the clouds above: when he strengthened the fountains of the deep: when he gave to the sea his decree, that the waters should not pass his commandment: when he appointed the foundations of the earth: then I was by him, as one brought up with him: and I was daily his delight, rejoicing always before him; rejoicing in the habitable part of his earth; and my delights were with the sons of men.

The first problem we have with this is the word that we know in KJV as "possessed." The original Hebrew word, *qanah*, was translated to the Greek word *ktizo* in the Septuagint (the Greek version of the Old Testament that was used during the era). This could mean either "possessed" or "begat." The latter meaning had been chosen by those who desired to use the passage to justify the pre-existence of the second person.

The second and more severe problem is the claim of what or who the word "me" indicates. But it is clear that the word "me" is wisdom in the form of a person—termed "personification." In the next couple of pages, I would like to address the reason why this is sensible. The trouble with the Greek interpretation is that neither Solomon, the rabbis, or common sense indicate that a second person or Christ is the one speaking. This doctrine emerged after the doctrine

The Development of the Trinity

of the trinity began to develop. It is a classic example of "eisegesis"—reading unintended meaning into the text.

Let us examine the theme of "wisdom" in the Book of Proverbs. Solomon used the word fifty-four times. His first mention is four times in the first chapter. In the middle of the chapter, Proverbs 1:20-33, we find these words:

> Wisdom crieth without; she uttereth her voice in the streets: she crieth in the chief place of concourse, in the openings of the gates: in the city she uttereth her words, saying, How long, ye simple ones, will ye love simplicity? and the scorners delight in their scorning, and fools hate knowledge? Turn you at my reproof: behold, I will pour out my spirit unto you, I will make known my words unto you. Because I have called, and ye refused; I have stretched out my hand, and no man regarded; but ye have set at nought all my counsel, and would none of my reproof: I also will laugh at your calamity; I will mock when your fear cometh; when your fear cometh as desolation, and your destruction cometh as a whirlwind; when distress and anguish cometh upon you. Then shall they call upon me, but I will not answer; they shall seek me early, but they shall not find me: for that they hated knowledge, and did not choose the fear of the LORD: they would none of my counsel: they despised all my reproof. Therefore shall they eat of the fruit of their own way, and be filled with their own devices. For the turning away of the simple

Part One: The New Doctrine Is Introduced

shall slay them, and the prosperity of fools shall destroy them. But whoso hearkeneth unto me shall dwell safely, and shall be quiet from fear of evil.

First, we read that wisdom is "crying out." Second, we see that wisdom (*Sophia* in the Greek version) is in the feminine. So the Son is a "she"? Both Clement of Alexandria[80] and Origen notice this:

For we must not, on account of their feminine name and nature, regard wisdom and righteousness as females; for these things are in our view the Son of God, as His genuine disciple has shown, when he said of Him, "Who of God is made to us wisdom, and righteousness, and sanctification, and redemption."[81]

Proverbs 3:13-18 (NIV) similarly speaks of wisdom:

Blessed is the man who finds wisdom, the man who gains understanding, for she is more profitable than silver and yields better returns than gold.

---

[80] Clement wrote, "The Father, by loving, became 'feminine'. The great proof of this is he whom he begot of Himself." It may be assumed that he is referring to Proverbs 8:22. (David Bercot, editor, *A Dictionary of Early Christian Beliefs* [Peabody, Mass: Hendrickson Publishers, 1998], 101.)

[81] *Origen against Celsus*, Book 5, Ch 39.

The Development of the Trinity

> She is more precious than rubies; nothing you desire can compare with her. Long life is in her right hand; in her left hand are riches and honor. Her ways are pleasant ways, and all her paths are peace. She is a tree of life to those who embrace her; those who lay hold of her will be blessed.

Again, wisdom is personified as female. The next chapter, Proverbs 4:6-9, again speaks of wisdom, saying, "Forsake her not. Love her. Exalt her. She shall promote thee. She shall bring thee to honour." Proverbs 7:4 reads: "Say unto wisdom, Thou art my sister; and call understanding thy kinswoman."

But it is not just a matter of gender. That cannot be the main concern. Perhaps, with a benefit of the doubt, Origen would have a point that the gender change does not matter. (His mentor, Clement does not have a solid point, though. See the footnote!) But, more importantly, what is wisdom doing? She is raising her voice in Proverbs 8:4-19:

> To you, O men, I call out; I raise my voice to all mankind. You who are simple, gain prudence; you who are foolish, gain understanding. Listen, for I have worthy things to say; I open my lips to speak what is right. My mouth speaks what is true, for my lips detest wickedness. All the words of my mouth are just; none of them is crooked or perverse. To the discerning all of them are right; they are faultless to those who have knowledge. Choose my instruction instead of silver, knowledge rather

Part One: The New Doctrine Is Introduced

than choice gold, for wisdom is more precious than rubies, and nothing you desire can compare with her. "I, wisdom, dwell together with prudence; I possess knowledge and discretion. To fear the LORD is to hate evil; I hate pride and arrogance, evil behavior and perverse speech. Counsel and sound judgment are mine; I have understanding and power. By me kings reign and rulers make laws that are just; by me princes govern, and all nobles who rule on earth. I love those who love me, and those who seek me find me. With me are riches and honor, enduring wealth and prosperity. My fruit is better than fine gold (NIV).

It should be obvious that this is a personification of wisdom. We can add to our understanding of this by noticing that other Jewish writings are similar. Ecclesiasticus 24 (This was not part of the canon but still is part of the Hebrew literature) reads:

Wisdom shall glory in the midst of her people; in the congregation of the Most High shall she open her mouth, and triumph before his power. I came out of the mouth of the Most High, and covered the earth as a cloud. I dwelt in the high places; I alone compassed the circuit of the heaven, and walked in the bottom of the deep, in the waves of the sea, and in all the earth. He created me from the beginning, before the world; and I shall never fail.

The Development of the Trinity

It should be obvious that Proverbs 8:22 is not speaking of Christ. Once again, the doctrine of a pre-existent second person was not in the mind of Solomon. Still, the trinitarian supporters look backward to Proverbs 8 to support the pre-existence of the Christ.

Adam Clarke, a well-known theologian of the late eighteenth and early nineteenth centuries, who wrote his volume that became the main commentary for the Methodist church for two hundred years, agreed fully that this passage does not reference Christ. In his commentary, he wrote:

> I have gone through this fine chapter. I am thoroughly satisfied that it speaks not one word either about the Divine or human nature of Christ. And I am fully persuaded, had there not been a preconceived creed, no soul of man, by fair criticism, would have ever found out that opinion.
>
> The WORD of God alone contains my creed. On a number of points I can go to the Greek and Latin fathers of the Church, to know what they believed, and the people of their respective communions believed; but . . . I have been shocked with reading over some things that have been written on [this] subject.
>
> I cannot believe their doctrine; I never did; I hope I never shall.[82]

---

[82] Adam Clarke, *Commentary of the Bible* (CD-Rom: Waco, Texas: Epiphany Software, 2006),

Part One: The New Doctrine Is Introduced

Well said, Mr. Clarke. When he commented on Proverbs 9 ("Wisdom hath builded her house. . . ."), he correctly wrote that this chapter is a "continuation of the parable begun in the preceding chapter, where wisdom is represented as a venerable lady."[83]

This should be sufficient for us. It is amazing that so many ministers have adopted the erroneous teachings that arose in the patristic era, for Christ was not the personified wisdom of Proverbs.

Justin Martyr (AD 100–165)

Without a doubt Justin, fully called Flavius Justinus, is the most representative writer of the onset of Greek philosophy merging with Christian revelation.[84] Justin was not officially ordained, but he was a popular teacher and writer. He was a philosopher before his conversion to Christianity, and continued to wear his cloak.[85] Justin Martyr "began the serious task of . . . making the religion seem respectable to

---

Proverbs 8.

[83] Ibid., Proverbs 9.

[84] Other well-known contributors to this era are Taitan and Theophilus of Antioch. The latter used a type of trinity (God, Logos, and wisdom) that was not as spelled out as later theories.

[85] Roger Olson and Adam English, *Pocket History of Theology* (Downers Grove, Ill.: InterVarsity Press, 2005), 15.

The Development of the Trinity

the Greeks by embracing their current philosophy."[86]

Justin combined his Christian faith with philosophy, particularly in regard to the Logos. It was with him that, as Grillmeier notes, the "Logos doctrine has a new lease of life."[87] In the words of Olson and English, he "explored and explained the concept of Christ as the Logos of God in order to explicate Christian beliefs."

Donald McKim writes:

> (Martyr) uses both biblical and philosophical language to describe God. He adopts the Greek *Logos* as a way to explain how the great gulf between God and humanity was bridged. . . . In Jesus Christ, the divine Logos "assumed shape and became a man." . . . Jesus as the Logos is distinct from the Father not only in name but also in number.[88]

Justin is quoted often in his "numerically distinct" theology. In *Second Apology*, he wrote:

---

[86] Ferm, ibid.

[87] Aloys Grillmeier, *Christ in the Christian Tradition*, Vol. I (New York: Sheed and Ward, 1964), 126.

[88] Donald K. McKim, *Theological Turning Points; Major Issues in Christian Thought* (Atlanta: John Knox Press, 1988) 9.

Part One: The New Doctrine Is Introduced

And that you may not change the [force of the] words just quoted, and repeat what your teachers assert,—either that God said to Himself, 'Let Us make,' just as we, when about to do something, oftentimes say to ourselves, 'Let us make;' or that God spoke to the elements, to wit, the earth and other similar substances of which we believe man was formed, 'Let Us make,'—I shall quote again the words narrated by Moses himself, from which we can indisputably learn that [God] conversed with some one who was numerically distinct from Himself, and also a rational Being.[89]

Justin used Genesis 1:26 ("Let us") as a support for the Son/Word as "another God."[90] Genesis 3:22 and 19:24 ("The LORD rained ... fire from the LORD") were also used to indicate there were "two in number."[91] Greek philosophy, in his opinion, was compatible with Scriptures. Kelly says that it was "apparently his sincere belief that the Greek thinkers had access to the works of Moses."[92]

Although the Word (Son) was still subordinated and not yet "co-equal" as in later developments, the groundwork

---

[89] Justin, *Second Apology*, Chapter 62, Schaff, *Early Church Fathers.*

[90] Quoted by Bernard, *Oneness and Trinity*, 67. Justin, *Dialogue with Tryhpho, a Jew.*

[91] *Dialogue*, 62 and 126.

[92] Kelly, *Doctrines*, 84.

The Development of the Trinity

for more distinctiveness of "persons" in the trinity had well been laid.

The new doctrine had been introduced.

Development Part Two: The New Doctrine Is Established

Many historians such as Ferm group four names as the "Anti-Gnostic[93] Fathers." Irenaeus and Tertullian were in the West, Clement and Origen in the East.[94] Bernard correctly better divides this age into three categories: Asia Minor (Irenaeus and Hippolytus), North Africa (Tertullian and Cyprian), and Alexandria (Clement and Origen).[95] This study will examine Irenaeus, Tertullian, Clement, and Origen. Then the theology of modalism will be defined and briefly examined.

Irenaeus (AD 130-202)

Many historians refer to this Bishop of Lyons (France) as the first post-apostolic theologian because of his

---

[93] Chalfant offers: "The anti-gnostic fathers are actually not very anti-gnostic other than their professed opposition to the outted Gnostics of their day."

[94] Ferm, 146.

[95] David Bernard, *A History of Christian Doctrine, The Post-Apostolic Age to the Middle Ages, AD 100-1500*, Vol. I (Hazelwood, Mo.: Word Aflame Press, 1995), 63-86.

The Development of the Trinity

purposeful stand "against heresies."[96] Polycarp may have influenced him, although it is doubtful whether it may be affirmed that Irenaeus was his actual disciple. His theology did not build upon that of Justin, although he did read his books.[97] When Irenaeus spoke of the Logos, he did not define the term as a separate "person."[98] The Logos was with God but only in the mind of God.

On the other hand, Irenaeus did speak of the preexistence of the Son:

> But the Son, eternally co-existing with the Father, from of old, yea, from the Creation, always reveals the Father to Angels, Archangels, Powers, Virtues, and all to whom He will that God should be revealed.[99]

His view of the Incarnation (calling it "recapitulation") took the forefront of his beliefs and teaching:

> The incarnation became, for Irenaeus, the key to the entire history of redemption and to personal

---

[96] This is the name of his most well-known work. It is in public domain, and can be accessed easily on the Internet.

[97] Bernard, *Oneness and Trinity*, 93.

[98] Ibid., 95.

[99] Irenaeus, *Against Heresies*, Ch. 30, #9. Schaff, *Early Church Fathers*.

Part Two: The New Doctrine Is Established

salvation. The incarnation itself is transformative, for it began a process of reversing the corruption of sin that results in alienation from God and death.[100]

Irenaeus, according to literature we have, at times used a type of threefold baptism ("We have received baptism for remission of sins in the name of God the Father, and in the name of Jesus Christ, the Son of God, who became incarnate and died and was raised, and in the Holy Spirit."[101]) but also quoted Acts 2:38 to teach that "believers are baptized into Jesus Christ for the remission of sins."[102] There is no indication, though, that he emphasized the name of Jesus over (or fulfilling) the triune formula.

Irenaeus's theology was that "after all has been completed and the mission of Christ is accomplished, Christ's special position in the economy of the Trinity will cease."[103] This reflects I Corinthians 15:24. Some of his language began to note three offices of God, but the word "trinity" had yet to appear.

In summary, Irenaeus stands in the middle of the Christology of the previous age and the Tertullian trinitarianism that was to be developed in the next age. Indeed,

---

[100] Olson, 18.

[101] Irenaeus, *Demonstration of Apostolic Preaching*, 3, Schaff, *Early Church Fathers*.

[102] Irenaeus, *Against Heresies*, III, Ch. 12:2, 4, 7, Schaff, *Early Church Fathers*.

[103] Heick, 109.

The Development of the Trinity

several passages are indicative of the rising movement of trinitarianism:

> Here [the Scripture] represents to us the Father addressing the Son; He who gave Him the inheritance of the heathen, and subjected to Him all His enemies. Since, therefore, the Father is truly Lord, and the Son truly Lord, the Holy Spirit has fitly designated them by the title of Lord. And again, referring to the destruction of the Sodomites, the Scripture says, "Then the LORD rained upon Sodom and upon Gomorrah fire and brimstone from the LORD out of heaven." For it here points out that the Son, who had also been talking with Abraham, had received power to judge the Sodomites for their wickedness. And this [text following] does declare the same truth: "Thy throne, O God, is for ever and ever; the sceptre of Thy kingdom is a right sceptre. Thou hast loved righteousness, and hated iniquity: therefore God, Thy God, hath anointed Thee." For the Spirit designates both [of them] by the name, of God—both Him who is anointed as Son, and Him who does anoint, that is, the Father.[104]

---

[104] Irenaeus, *Against Heresies*, III, Ch. 3, 6, Schaff, *Early Church Fathers*. The words in brackets, of course, are summaries of condensed phrases. Some of his theology should be fine, but the Son pre-existing as the judge in Sodom is not biblical.

Part Two: The New Doctrine Is Established

Tertullian (AD 160-220)

Tertullian, a lawyer and then presbyter in Carthage, North Africa, plays the most important part in this puzzle. He is commonly regarded as the "father" of the concept and word "trinity." He spoke of the *trinitas* (Latin for "trinity") as being "distinct" *personae*, persons. Like the Greek Apologists, he said the Word was inherent in God. However, he also said that Christ became a distinct person at a point of time (before Bethlehem's miracle). This was a developing concept, as Berkhof writes:

> Tertullian takes his starting-point in the doctrine of the Logos, but develops it in a way that became historically significant . . . . The Logos is . . . an independent Person . . . . There was a time when he was not.[105] . . . He enlarged the doctrine of the Logos into a doctrine of the Trinity.[106]

It is common knowledge that Tertullian did not identify the persons to be co-equal and co-existent but taught that the Son was subordinate to the Father.[107] In *Against Hermonogenes* he wrote against the co-equality of the Son and the Father.

---

[105] This comment predates Arius, who was known later for this saying being part of his "song."

[106] Berkhof, 65.

[107] Berkhof, 63.

He could not have been the Lord of a substance which was co-equal with Himself (Chapter 9).

No one thing is the exact mirror of another thing; this is to say, it is not its co-equal (Chapter 40).

In other chapters of the same document, Tertullian argued against co-eternality!

What God, then, is He who subjects me to a contemporaneous, co-eternal power (Chapter 7)?

That what is eternal cannot possibly admit of diminution and subjection, so as to be considered inferior to another co-eternal Being (Chapter 15).

Tertullian's concept of "subordinationalism" is regarded today by trinitarians as heretical. This is amazing. Here we have a revered "father" of the major Catholic-Christian doctrine of the Godhead, whose concept is now regarded as false! Regarding baptism, he notably used Matthew 28:19, "into the Father, the Son, and the Holy Spirit—not into a unipersonal God."[108] Tertullian baptized,

---

[108] David Bercot, ed., *A Dictionary of Early Christian Beliefs* (Peabody, Mass: Hendrickson Publishers, 1998), 57.

Part Two: The New Doctrine Is Established

however, three times—one for each "person"![109]

It is interesting that Tertullian said he refused the mixture of Greek philosophy to Christian theology.[110] (His famous question was: "What does Athens have to do with Jerusalem?" In other words, why should we mix carnal philosophy with supernatural revelation?) According to his statements, the distinctiveness of the persons is not drawn from Greek thinking but from the Scripture. Yet in spite of Tertullian's protests against philosophy, most historians dispute that. Kelly amazingly states that Tertullian "followed the Apologists" rather than Scripture in dating the Son before the nativity.[111]

Tertullian's most well-known treatise is *Against Praxeas*,[112] in which he battles modalistic monarchianism, which was similar to Oneness.

Tertullian argued clearly for the Son's pre-existence:

---

[109] Kelly, *Creeds*, 45. Kelly reports the above, and then adds: "The only conclusion a fair-minded critic can draw is that Tertullian knew nothing of a declaratory creed used in baptism." Yet it appears that Bercot (above) thinks that this baptism was in direct contradiction to baptism in the name of Jesus.

[110] Olson and English, 20-21.

[111] Kelly, *Doctrines*, 112.

[112] Historians are not sure if he was writing against a person named Praxeas or if he was using the name Praxeas to represent the meaning "busybody." I suspect the former because of Tertullian's personal, polemic tone in the document.

The Development of the Trinity

It is the Son, therefore, who has been from the beginning administering judgment, throwing down the haughty tower, and dividing the tongues, punishing the whole world by the violence of waters, raining upon Sodom and Gomorrah fire and brimstone, as the LORD from the LORD. For He it was who at all times came down to hold converse with men, from Adam on to the patriarchs and the prophets, in vision, in dream, in mirror, in dark saying; ever from the beginning laying the foundation of the course of His dispensations, which He meant to follow out to the very last. Thus was He ever learning even as God to converse with men upon earth, being no other than the Word which was to be made flesh.[113]

Tertullian's means of proof is ludicrous, although he was not the only trinitarian to use Genesis 19:24 as a support.[114] During the time of this writing, Tertullian had al-

---

[113] Ibid., ch. 16. This writing was composed to "prove" the case against the modalists—"showing" that God had a separate Son in the Old Testament.

[114] Genesis 19:24 had been previously used by Justin, Irenaeus, and later Novatian and Athanasius. Finis Dake in his early-twentieth-century commentary on Genesis 19:24 also wrote: "This is a clear example of more than one Jehovah. One Jehovah on earth rained fire and brimstone from another Jehovah in

Part Two: The New Doctrine Is Established

ready left the "mainstream" of the "catholic" (this word originally meant "universal") church to joint the Montanists, probably in AD 207.[115] It is amazing. Once again, we state this: Here we have a "founding father" who was not a part of the main church and whose doctrines are still questioned. Yet his influence on the trinity had been firmly set.

Clement of Alexandria (AD 150–215)

On the "opposite end,"[116] both geographically and theologically, we find Clement in the Alexandrian school. The Alexandrian school was the center of Christian scholarship in the East. It was led first by Clement in AD 190 and

---

heaven." He went as far as to say that there were "two Jehovahs" (Commentary on Isaiah 40:3, referring to the Genesis 19:24 passage).

Adam Clarke notes that "many of the primitive fathers and several modern divines" pointed to two persons in Genesis 19:24 but comments that the passage is certainly not a proof. Clarke, later in his comments on Colossians 1:16-17, wrote: "It is impossible that there can be two or more Omnipotents, Infinites, or Eternals. The text says that all things were made BY him and FOR him, which is a demonstration that the apostle understood Jesus Christ to be truly and essentially God."

[115] González, 180.

[116] Olson and English, 19. In other words, the East used philosophy freely and admittedly.

The Development of the Trinity

then by Origen in AD 202.[117] The school, influenced unashamedly by Platonic philosophy, sought to find allegorical meanings in the Scriptures.[118] Kelly remarks:

> In the East where the intellectual climate was impregnated with Neo-Platonic ideas about the hierarchy of being, an altogether different,[119] confessedly pluralistic approach had established itself.[120]

Ferm writes that Clement was a "Christian Neo-Platonist, heavy in emphasis upon the doctrine of the logos."[121] González writes that the "Hellenistic Judaism that followed in the tradition of Philo" found itself in both Clement and Origen.[122] Although Clement stated that he believed the Scriptures are inspired by God,[123] he also admit-

---

[117] Stanley J. Grenz, David Guetzki, and Cherith Fee Nordling, *Pocket Dictionary of Theological Terms* (Downers Grove, Ill.: InterVarsity Press, 1999), 8.

[118] Ironically, however, Origen took the Scripture (Matthew 19:12) literally and castrated himself!

[119] Kelly's word "different" compares the East with the West's more monarchian approach.

[120] Kelly, *Doctrines*, 136. Is Kelly admitting to error when he uses the word "confessedly"?

[121] Ferm, 150.

[122] González, 193.

[123] Ibid., 199.

Part Two: The New Doctrine Is Established

ted being a "keen student of Plato, Pythagoras, Zeno, and Aristotle,"[124] and explained Christ in terms of the Logos[125] as Justin did.

Clement "takes Christ's pre-existence prior to the incarnation for granted,"[126] not as God, but "like all other souls."[127] "This Logos-filled soul assumed a body, and even this body was penetrated and 'divinized' by the Logos."[128] This could mean that Jesus was not human, and was a divine being that was manifest to the world. This touches on Docetism,[129] a Christological theology that he "did not entirely avoid."[130] In summary, Clement had no problems with equating Christ with the pre-existent Logos, even though it was built upon Greek philosophy.

Origen (AD 185–254)

Origen had an even greater and more lasting influence in Alexandria than Clement. He "developed a system

---

[124] Richardson, 43.

[125] Ibid.

[126] Ibid.

[127] Berkhof, 73.

[128] Ibid.

[129] Docetism believed that Christ's body was only an illusion.

[130] Berkhof, ibid.

The Development of the Trinity

of Christian philosophy on a larger scale."[131] He "learned the Platonic philosophy and he set out to wed the Christian faith to it."[132] He did not mind combining the Scriptures with philosophy. As an example, He felt that the thrice-holy passage in the sixth chapter of Isaiah was "to inspire generations of Greek theologians."[133] He "ended up unwittingly accepting and teaching some ideas that seem more consistent with pagan philosophy and culture than with the teachings of Moses, Paul, and other apostles."[134]

His teaching on the pre-existence of the soul[135] is remarkable. The soul of a person was formed before the body was formed.[136] Fallen spirits, which originally were co-equal and co-eternal with each other, later became souls and were clothed with bodies.[137] Since every person was already formed before birth, we perhaps see where the idea of the pre-existence of Christ came from. However, Christ in his theory is not just a man but a deity.

According to Heick, Origen was the first writer[138] to

---

[131] Ferm, 150.

[132] Ibid.

[133] Kelly, *Doctrines*, 131.

[134] Olson and English, 26.

[135] Berkhof, 73.

[136] Bercot, 489.

[137] Ibid.

[138] Bernard, *Oneness and Trinity*, 112. Although Bernard suggests this, Heick thinks that his

Part Two: The New Doctrine Is Established

clearly teach the eternal trinity of persons. He taught that the Logos was a person "from all eternity."[139] Kelly says that the "underlying structure of thought is unmistakably borrowed from contemporary Platonism," particularly in its parallel ideas of the world of co-eternal spiritual beings.[140] Yet the question would arise: How could the Son be a "son" if there were a Father who was not before Him?

Origen proposed this answer: The Son was "eternally generated." He further explained, "His generation is as eternal and everlasting as the brilliancy produced by the Sun."[141] Also: "The Father did not beget the Son and set Him free after He was begotten, but He is always begetting Him."[142] With this theory of eternal generation, Origen was able to subordinate Christ/Logos and yet have Him exist from all eternity.[143] This makes no sense, though, to logic; it is, in the words of Bible commentator Adam Clarke, a

---

teaching was "unconsciously a step in the direction of co-eternality and co-equality of the persons of the Trinity" (Heick, 146).

[139] Heick, 146.

[140] Kelly, *Doctrines*, 131.

[141] Origen, *De Principiis*, 1, 2, 4, Schaff *Early Church Fathers*.

[142] Ibid.

[143] Richardson, 44.

The Development of the Trinity

self-contradiction.[144] Years later Barton Stone (Cane Ridge revival of 1801) would write that it is indeed an "incomprehensible" mystery![145]

The history of dogma now would rest more upon Origen than Clement.[146] Harnack sees that this new theology "bears unmistakable marks of Neo-Platonism and Gnosticism," and "speculated in the manner of Justin."[147] Most historians such as Pelikan consider Origen as the primary developer of the Logos-equals-Son doctrine.[148] At the same time, subordination was still part of the Son's role.[149] That may seem confusing, but the "eternally generated" Son was still the Son in his role to the Father.

Origen could speak of the Son both as a creature of the Father and thus subordinate to the Father, while also saying that the Father and the Son are of the same substance. "The Son . . . is described as a 'secondary God' to whom prayer should not be directed. . . . While he indicates the differences between the members of the Trinity, he is

---

[144] We will have more on his comments in the section on the pre-existence of Christ.

[145] Barton Stone, *The Biography of Eld. Barton Stone, Written by Himself* (New York: Arno Press, 1847), 13.

[146] Harnack, 331.

[147] Ibid.

[148] Pelikan, 191.

[149] Ibid.

Part Two: The New Doctrine Is Established

not as clear on how they are united."[150]

Chalfant notes, "This 'eternalized' the subordinated 'God the Son' by means of his begetting, even though the later trinitarian theologians attempted to equalize the Son dogmatically."[151] There were obvious ambiguities in Origen. He both "cleared and muddied the waters of Christian teaching, so that decades after his death his troubling legacy . . . erupted in the greatest controversy in the history of Christian theology."[152] Before we come to this "eruption," we will examine a theological "reaction."[153]

---

[150] McKim, 13.

[151] Chalfant, ibid.

[152] Origen's theology was eventually condemned as heretical at the Second Council of Constantinople in AD 553.

[153] McKim, 11. McKim uses the term "reaction." Not all scholars will agree that this was a "reaction" since the foundation of the Church was monotheistic. Nevertheless, the term "modalism" did not appear until the late second century. While the theology may not have been new, the term was. In comparison, the term "Pentecostals" has not been used through all ages, but the term identified nineteenth-century (and identifies current) Christians who believe the church was begun on the Day of Pentecost with its Pentecostal power, not just by the regeneration of faith. In like manner, the term "modalism" identified Christians who were clearly reacting to the developing trinitarian theology.

The Development of the Trinity

Modalism

Two theologies fall under the general umbrella of monarchianism. Dynamic monarchianism defended the monarch, or monad, or unity of God yet denied the deity of Christ. It proposed a type of "adoptionism"[154]—Christ was adopted when the Spirit fell on him at his baptism. The most noteworthy proponent was Paul of Samosata.

The more popular version,[155] though, was modalistic monarchianism, or modalism. In the Western theologically centripetal city of Rome,[156] the doctrine was the official theory for almost a generation,[157] taking in the Romans bishops Victor to Callixtus.[158] Heick says, "The chief interest of Modalism was to maintain Christian monotheism without sacrificing the divinity of Christ."[159] He continues: "The earliest literary defenders of Modalism were markedly monothe-

---

[154] McKim, 29.

[155] Heick, 152.

[156] Ibid., 147.

[157] Harnack, 52. Also, Tertullian stated that the modalists were "in the majority" in his *Against Praxeas*, although Gregory Boyd and others contend that we cannot base our facts on this remark alone.

[158] Heick, 151.

[159] Ibid., 149.

Part Two: The New Doctrine Is Established

istic, and had a real interest in Biblical Christianity."[160]

The main defenders of this doctrine also preached against the eternal Logos=Christ teaching. The champions included Noetus, Praxeas,[161] and finally Sabellius.[162] The most well known were Praxeas and Sabellius. In the aforementioned *Against Praxeas*, we obtain much of our information about the modalists. The friction between Tertullian and the modalists may easily be detected in excerpts such as the following remarks of Tertullian:

> They are constantly throwing out against us that we are preachers of two gods and three gods, while they take to themselves pre-eminently the credit worshippers of the One God. . . . "We," say they, "maintain the Monarchy."[163]

This sounds like something that could have been written more recently![164] The general teachings of the modalists are said to be this: God was one person but was

---

[160] Ibid.

[161] The possibility of his not being a real person was mentioned earlier.

[162] All historians agree that the Roman bishops, from Victor to Callixtus, were modalists.

[163] *Against Praxeas*, 3.

[164] The famed debate of 1916 in the Assemblies of God could have recorded almost the same words!

The Development of the Trinity

acting in three different "modes." At times they have been represented (misrepresented?) as putting God in masks. (However, we don't know if this was exactly their teaching; it seems to have been exaggerated by trinitarian historians.[165]) Pelikan remarks:

> Both monotheism and the deity of Christ were safeguarded, but there remained no distinction between Father, Son, and Holy Spirit. This theory "thinks it impossible to believe in one God unless it says that the Father and Son and Holy Spirit are one and the same."[166]

Again, that may be an exaggeration. The modalists did not care to define the different "personhoods" of the three functions of God, especially in non-biblical terms.

Such terms (such as "co-equal, co-eternal, God the Son, and God the Holy Ghost") may have been just beginning their development, and we can imagine, if so, that the modalists would likely have refused their use.

The modalists were often accused of "Patripassianism"—the thought that the Father suffered. Since the Greek thinking was that God was distant from us, how could God Himself suffer? It would only, in their minds, be the

---

[165] This problem is covered in detail in William Chalfant's *Sabellius: His Life and Theology*.

[166] Pelikan, 178. He is quoting from *Against Praxeas*, 2.

Logos/Son who could suffer. But we do find that Paul would also be accused of Patripassianism: "God was in Christ, reconciling the world unto himself" (II Corinthians 5:19). The prophet Zachariah would also be accused of the same error: "They shall look upon me whom they have pierced" (Zechariah 12:10).

Sabellius, arriving later on the scene than the first modalists, is usually considered the most significant of them.[167] He wrote at least five books, but they have been lost or destroyed. It would be of great interest to find them. Sabellius has been accused by some to have taught a somewhat strange theory: The Father, Son, and Spirit had successive roles, not occupied simultaneously.[168] If this theology was taught, it was not biblical. I would think that this was not his theology. Pelikan remarks, in fact, that this may be a "somewhat dubious report."[169]

The Council of Nicea (AD 325)

Different views of the Godhead and Christology were about to collide. What do we do with this man called Jesus? Kelly asks: "Was He fully divine, in the precise sense of the term. . . . Or was He after all a creature, superior no doubt to the rest of creation?"[170]

---

[167] Pelikan, 150.

[168] Heick, 150.

[169] Pelikan, 179.

[170] Kelly, *Doctrines*, 223.

The Development of the Trinity

These were the questions that filled the minds of the emerging "Catholic" church. No event has been so historically regarded as a turning point as the first "ecumenical" council in Nicea. As we will see, this council produced a creed that was more "modalistic" in its first "edition." But since it was the first of seven councils, it should be considered a watershed event for the Catholic church, just by the mere virtue of its existence.

From Nero to Diocletian, the church (both Apostolic and Catholic) had suffered persecutions. Finally, in the year AD 313, Emperor Constantine (with his then co-emperor Licinius[171]) declared an end to the trouble at the Edict of Milan. He had supposedly seen a sign of the cross in the sky, accompanied by the words: "In this sign conquer." Although he was not baptized until near his death, he professed Christianity and wanted peace in his kingdom. His motive was unity between politics and religion.

Arius, a priest[172] in charge of a church in Alexandria, had arguments with his bishop Alexander over the divinity of Christ. His song was heard throughout Alexandria:

> Arius of Alexandria, I'm the talk of all the town,
> Friend of saints, elect of heaven,
> filled with learning and renown;
> If you want the Logos doctrine,

---

[171] Bernard, *Oneness and Trinity*, 44.

[172] Some have referred to him as a presbyter (Heick, 154).

Part Two: The New Doctrine Is Established

> I can serve it hot and not:
> God begat him and before he was begotten,
> He was not.[173]

The last words rang strongly, even causing riots in the streets.[174] There was a "time when He was not." He was born in time (before, but not at Bethlehem). Arius believed that Christ could not be the Father, but was still a creature— a sort of demi-god. Arius believed in an absolute distinctiveness of the Father and the Son, using Scriptures such as Proverbs 8:22-31 that had already been (improperly) exegeted by Origen's pupil, Dionysius of Alexandria.[175] In a nutshell, the "Son, to Arius, was God, but not divine."[176] But this cannot be. If He was not divine, He could not be God. His theories were probably similar to today's Jehovah's Witnesses.

The quarrels ripped the Alexandrian church with such violence that Emperor Constantine felt that he should intervene. He sent Bishop Hosius of Cordova to Alexandria to settle the issues, but the bishop came back with news that the trouble was still alive.[177] Constantine then planned the famous Nicean meeting, paying for the travel, food, and lodging of the bishops. Even today's society would count

---

[173] McKim, 15.

[174] Ibid.

[175] Pelikan, 192.

[176] Heick, 155.

[177] Richardson, 52.

The Development of the Trinity

this odd. This was even more so in that day—the Christians had been persecuted and mutilated by unbelievers; now they would have affinity together. With only twelve years passing between Milan's edict and Nicea's meeting, compromise was at least on the way.

Most historians count 318 bishops and their representatives from the East[178] who attended the council. Athanasius, the arch-deacon[179] of Alexander, was there and ended up playing a major role. He is regarded as the "Father of Trinitarian orthodoxy."[180]

Eusibius of Nicodemia presented an Arianistic creed, but it was voted out. Eusibius of Caesarea offered his creed of the "Logos of God," which was also rejected. Finally, Hosius offered the word *homoousios*—of one substance in referring to Christ and the Father. This turned out to be fundamental in the Nicene Creed that was adopted. (This term had already been used in guarding the identification of Jesus Christ as God.)

Athanasius is credited with taking the lead in the battle, though he had been exiled five times. All but two of the bishops signed the creed, and the two who abstained

---

[178] Later the West was also influenced by Athanasian theology, much by Hilary of Potier, the "Athanasius of the West"(Richardson, 55).

[179] Heick, 156. The "arch-deacon" is Heick's word. Some historians refer to him simply as a deacon.

[180] Bernard, *Oneness and Trinity*, 174.

Part Two: The New Doctrine Is Established

were sent into exile.[181]

Besides the phrase "of one substance with the Father," the English meaning of the word *homoousios*, insisted upon by Alexander,[182] the creed offered important wording: "Begotten not made." "Begotten" is a biblical word, but "not made" was more "doctrinally specific."[183] This mindset reflects the erroneous theology that Jesus was "begotten" —sometime in eternity—but not "made" at Bethlehem.

We must pause here to reflect what has been often taught. Many modern historians declare that the "Nicene doctrine of the Trinity stands midway between Tritheism and Sabellianism."[184] This is a great "straw man" approach. For example, Philip Schaff writes:

> Many passages of the Nicene fathers have unquestionably a tritheistic sound, but are neutralized by

---

[181] J.W.C. Wand, *The Four Councils* (Great Britain, Faith Press, Ltd., 1951), 12.

[182] Olson and English, 32.

[183] Ibid. They remarked that this is "nowhere used in Scripture," but Paul did say the Son of God was "made of a woman" in Galatians 4:4, KJV. Most other versions of this passage, though, read "born of a woman." See also Hebrew 2:14.

[184] Philip Schaff, *History of the Christian Church, Vol. III: Nicene and Post-Nicene Christianity: From Constantine the Great to Gregory the Great, AD 311-300* (Grand Rapids: Eerdmans Publishing Company, 1910), 669.

The Development of the Trinity

others which by themselves may bear a Sabellian construction, so that their position must be regarded as midway between these two extremes.[185]

I'm not sure it is that simple, however. The issue at hand was Arianism, which denied Christ's deity. Its author, Arius, believed that Christ could not be fully God but was a sort of pre-existent demi-god. In reaction, the Nicene Creed exalted Christ as the "very God of very God" without establishing the persons' relationships within the trinity.

So the Nicene Creed was not originally meant as a compromise at all. It was a rebuke—a refutation—to the two-person theory of Arius. To most of the trinitarians-to-be (pre-existent Logos equals the pre-existent Son), the complaint after the creed was that *homoousios* was too modalistic, and changes were on the way for the next council.

The Council of Constantinople (AD 381)

Emperor Theodosius called a new council at Constantinople. A revised version of the Nicene Creed was written. The original Nicene Creed ended with an "anathema," a curse to those who did not believe the same. Also missing from this first creed was a defining of the role of the Holy Spirit, which heretofore had not been much considered nor debated. In 381, the council at Constantinople completed the "Niceno-Constantinople" Creed. The condemnatory phrase was gone, but the Holy Spirit portion was

---

[185] Schaff, 674.

Part Two: The New Doctrine Is Established

added. A more important phrase was also added. The Son was begotten of the Father "before all ages."

As more modern trinitarian apologists such as Calvin Beisner would record, the majority of Christendom would write that the "Niceno-Constantinopolitan" Creed is "an accurate representation of the teaching of the New Testament."[186] Beisner also writes that "most cannot understand its definitions or implications."[187] How can something be accepted that cannot be understood? Most modern trinitarian preachers answer that the matter must be "taken by faith." It is not revelatory faith the illuminates the mind and the spirit. It is faith that—in the vernacular of our modern age's young people—would say, "Well, whatever!" Should we just "accept" something and then call it "faith"?

A major problem with the new Creed was and is the pre-existence of Christ. We have touched on this but now will more fully examine this issue.

The Pre-existence of Christ

"The pre-existence of Christ," writes theologian Douglas McCready, "is not a doctrine most people give

---

[186] E. Calvin Beisner, *God in Three Persons* (Wheaton: Tyndale House Publishers, 1984), 7.

[187] Ibid., 18. Beisner comments that "many ... hold a modalistic conception of the Trinity, at least unconsciously." In other words, the revelation of God in Christ surely comes to every believer, even though the pollution of the ages will try to darken the light.

The Development of the Trinity

much thought to."[188] Yet he admits that it is "a part of the foundation of Christian faith on which these other doctrines depend."[189] If a doctrine is something that has not been considered yet is foundational to subsequent faith, the concept should be closely re-examined.

The pre-existence of Christ was not in the original Nicene Creed. It was added some time between Nicea (325) and Constantinople (381). The addition is shown in italics:

> And in one Lord Jesus Christ . . . begotten of the Father *before all worlds*: Light of Light, very God of very God, begotten, not made, being of one substance with the Father;[190]

Note the new words: "before all worlds." According to McCready, "Justin Martyr (had) identified the preexistent Christ with the 'angel of the Lord' in the Old Testament, and Novatian had concluded that Abraham's visitor on the eve of Sodom's destruction was the same pre-existent Christ."[191] This would make Jesus to be a pre-Bethlehem

---

[188] Douglass McCready, "He Came Down from Heaven: The Preexistence of Christ Revisited," *Journal of the Evangelical Theological Society* 40/3 September 1997, 419.

[189] Ibid.

[190] The full wording of both creeds is found on pages 97-99.

[191] McCready, 421.

Part Two: The New Doctrine Is Established

soul separate from God. Later Origen, who was "a firm exponent of the theory of the pre-existence of all souls,"[192] thought that Christ was also pre-existent. Once again, the Nicene writers did not include this theology, but the Constantinopolitan authors did.

E. Calvin Beisner, in his support of the trinity and its development, defends the words: "Begotten of the Father before all worlds":

> That is, his generation must be from eternity. There never was a time when he was not, for even before all ages he was the Son of God. The Word, the Son, therefore, is eternal (John 1:1-3, Hebrews 13:8, John 8:58).

His generation "must be" from eternity? If he means that Christ was eternally begotten, he is quoting Origen.

Perhaps the confusion of eternal pre-existence stems from the mixing of the Word and the Son. The Word is eternal and is a part of God. The Word is with God yet is God. The Son, however, is the "Word made flesh," not the pre-existent Son made flesh.

Adam Clarke recognized and addressed the problem of pre-incarnation. His commentary on Luke 1:52 states:

> To say that he was begotten from all eternity is, in my opinion, absurd; and the phrase eternal Son is

---

[192] J.N.D. Kelly, *Early Christian Doctrines* (London: Adam and Charles Black, 1958), 180.

The Development of the Trinity

a positive self-contradiction. ETERNITY is that which has had no beginning, nor stands in any reference to TIME. SON supposes time, generation, and father; and time also antecedent to such generation. Therefore the conjunction of these two terms, Son and eternity, is absolutely impossible, as they imply essentially different and opposite ideas.[193]

"Absurd" is a strong word for Clarke, but he could not have said it better. He also went on to say that John Wesley had examined and agreed with his opinions. Charles Wesley was also in agreement.[194]

---

[193] Adam Clarke, *Commentary of the Bible* (CD-Rom: Waco, Texas: Epiphany Software, 2006), Luke 1:52.

[194] Clarke's commentary on Hebrews 1:8: "On the doctrine of the eternal Sonship of the Divine nature of Christ I once had the privilege of conversing with the late reverend John Wesley, about three years before his death; he read from a book in which I had written the argument against this doctrine. He did not attempt to reply to it; but allowed that, on the ground on which I had taken it, the argument was conclusive. I observed that the proper, essential Divinity of Jesus Christ appeared to me to be so absolutely necessary to the whole Christian scheme, and to the faith both of penitent sinners and saints, that it was of the utmost importance to set it in the clearest and strongest point of view; and that, with my present light, I could not

Part Two: The New Doctrine Is Established

When did this new theological terminology "before all worlds" take root? Between Nicea and Constantinople there were about twelve minor councils. We find the creed's addition had appeared by the time of one of them: the Council of Antioch in 341.[195] It is very possible that the addition was made at that time by Gregory, one of the Cappadocians. In any case, we do know that it was added into the second council's creed.

We have seen now that the doctrine of the trinity was introduced and established, especially in the last council. Since this last major council, Constantinople, was so influenced by the Cappadocians, we should backtrack and look at their influence.

The Cappadocians

The Cappadocians gave the trinity the meaning that would last into the Middle Ages. Building "on the foundation of Origen,"[196] they established "the doctrine of the

---

credit it, if I must receive the common doctrine of the Sonship of the Divine nature of our Lord. He mentioned two eminent divines who were of the same opinion."

[195] Schaff, *History of the Christian Church*, Vol. III, 660 (footnote 1).

[196] Adolph Harnack, *History of Dogma*, Vol. IV, trans. Neil Buchanan (New York: Dover Publications, 1961), 121.

The Development of the Trinity

Trinity that remained the dominant one in the Church."[197] Basil (329-379), his brother Gregory of Nyssa (d. 386), and their friend Gregory of Nazianzus (325-381), all received liberal educations[198] and were the theological thinkers of the fourth century, setting the tone for later.[199] Many historians have commented that they used the ideas of Plato, Aristotle,[200] and Origen[201] to help form their ideas.

Basil of Caesarea

Basil, with a "model drawn from logic,"[202] described God as the trinity. According to the respected historian Jaroslav Pelikan, he "unabashedly" borrowed ideas from "the more advanced philosophers."[203] He saw the three persons as co-equal and co-eternal. Most importantly in the

---

[197] Ibid., 119.

[198] Anthony Meredith, *The Cappodocians* (Crestwood, New York: St. Vladimer's Seminary Press, 2000), 7.

[199] Ibid., viii.

[200] Ibid., x.

[201] Ibid., 10.

[202] Ibid., 105.

[203] Jaroslav Pelikan, *The Christian Tradition; A History of the Development of Doctrine; Vol. I: The Emergence of the Catholic Tradition (100-600)* (Chicago: University of Chicago Press, 1971), 221.

Part Two: The New Doctrine Is Established

story of the trinity's development, the idea of the Holy Spirit joining the other two "persons" began also in Basil:

> Everybody admits that the Father is God and the Son is God. But we always unite the Spirit with the two other members of the Trinity in our prayers and hymns, and above all our doxologies. Persons so conjointly honored must share a common nature. To deny the Spirit's deity is to put a question beside that of Father and Son.[204]

This was a new idea. Of course, if the Father and the Son were co-equal and co-eternal "persons," why not the Spirit as well?[205] What began as defining the Father and the Son was now lent to the Spirit: They must all be persons.

Were there arguments against Basil? There must have been, since we know that Basil authored a defensive work treatise entitled, *"Against Those Who Falsely Accuse Us of Saying That There Are Three Gods."*[206] Although I could not find an actual copy of his words, we do see by the

---

[204] Meredith, 33.

[205] Yet at the same time he was "reticent about the actual assertion of deity and consubstantiality of all three persons," Meredith continues. (In Letter 71 to Gregory of Nazianzus, he defends his reluctance to worship the Holy Spirit in the same way as the Father.) Yet the idea had begun.

[206] Pelikan, 221. It would be interesting and historically informative to find the actual document.

The Development of the Trinity

title that there were those that defended the monarchy (the mighty God in Christ) against Basil.

"Apparently," Pelikan writes in his observation of Basil's theology, "the monotheistic confession of Deuteronomy 6:4, which Christianity had inherited from Judaism, seemed to be at stake." Basil founded his doctrine in the baptismal formula of Matthew 28:19, saying "it was Christ, not orthodoxy" that put the persons side by side.[207] That is remarkable, since Matthew 28:19 had not been employed in the trinitarian fashion for one hundred years after Jesus arose. The very scene of Christ's resurrection and opening of the mind to His deity now became the defense of three persons. In Basil's era, the liturgy had been "Glory be to the Father through the Son and in the Holy Spirit." Basil, however, changed the words: "Glory be to the Father with the Son together with the Holy Spirit."[208] He distinguished and eternalized three different persons. He was clearly laying the foundation for words like "co-equal" and "co-eternal" to be "established" beyond repair.

Gregory of Nyssa

Gregory of Nyssa used Greek thinking and that of Origen.[209] His influence at the Council of Antioch indicated

---

[207] Pelikan, 217.

[208] Ibid.

[209] Meredith, 54. Harnack (see previous reference) connected Origen to the Cappadocians in

Part Two: The New Doctrine Is Established

his strong avocation of the "eternal distinction among the three persons of the Trinity."[210] As stated earlier, it was most likely at this council that we find the "before all ages" mentioned in the Nicene Creed. As previously stated, it appears very likely that the addition of the words came from Gregory of Nyssa. At the very least, he was supportive of the concept.

Gregory identified the "Father as the source of power, the Son as the power of the Father, and the Holy Spirit as the Spirit of power."[211] Gregory often remarked that we should "guard the traditions we have received from the fathers, as ever sure and immovable, and seek from the Lord a means of defending our faith." He was building on the faith he had received in the traditions of the Catholic church.[212] What was beforehand only speculation and philosophy was now becoming indisputable doctrine.

Gregory of Nyssa even compared the three persons

---

general; Meredith points specifically to Gregory of Nyssa.

[210] Ibid., 5. Schaff (see previous reference) thought that it was at the Council of Antioch that the group of words "before all worlds" was added. Meredith agrees with this, pointing out the presence of Gregory of Nyssa at this council.

[211] Pelikan, 223.

[212] The subordinational Son (the Father unbegotten, and the Son begotten) of Tertullian's thinking was now being changed.

The Development of the Trinity

to Peter, James, and John.[213] Today this would be considered to be a crude illustration of the Godhead and would, as well put by Pelikan, "invoke the cry of Tritheism from most readers."[214] Oddly enough, Augustine saw no problem with the same illustration of the Godhead.[215] We'll get to him soon. But the development goes on.

Gregory of Nazianzus

Gregory of Nazianzus also was considered a "follower of Origen and Plato."[216] Gregory played three special roles in the trinitarian development.

First, he put more insistence on the deity of the Holy Spirit than the other two.[217] The role of the Holy Spirit had been somewhat neglected in the first development of the trinity, but now that the Father and Son were co-equal, the Holy Spirit, now regarded more as a "person," should also

---

[213] Pelikan, 220.

[214] Ibid.

[215] "But since three men appeared, and no one of them is said to be greater than the rest either in form, or age, or power, why should we not here understand, as visibly intimated by the visible creature, the equality of the Trinity, and one and the same substance in three persons?" (Augustine, *On the Trinity*, Book II, Ch. 11, also in Ch 18.)

[216] Meredith, 43.

[217] Ibid., 106.

be regarded equal with the other two.[218] The silence, which had been "a source of considerable embarrassment,"[219] had now been broken. Now the discussion was on; the third person would receive "due honor."

Second, he was bishop for a short while at Constantinople. Although he died the year before the council of 381,[220] his influence was obvious to the new philosophy.

Third, he had the most profound effect of the three Cappadocians, through his writings, on Augustine.

Summary of Cappadocians

Before we go to Augustine, we recap the development of the Cappadocians. Although each member differed slightly, through them the major trinitarian concepts took root. The Cappadocian teaching was beginning to be

> ... enshrined in the liturgy and, if one reads them right, *"documented" in the Scriptures*. Now it was the task of theology to defend it, and to reflect upon it. In one sense, the dogma of the Trinity was

---

[218] Pelikan, 221.

[219] Ibid., 212. Amphilochius of Iconium wrote in 376 "the Holy Spirit had not been discussed" in regards to its deity (ibid., 211).

[220] Or he died in the same year, depending upon the historian.

The Development of the Trinity

the end result of theology.[221]

As Professor TeSelle states, the trinity could now be "documented." The pre-existent Christ was now traditionally recognized, and the "persons" were actually separate, co-equal, and co-existent.

The new doctrine was established.

---

[221] Eugene TeSelle, *Augustine* (Nashville: Abingdon Press, 2006), 46. Italics and quote marks are mine.

Development Part Three: The New Doctrine Is Mandated

What began as conjecture now was doctrine. The preliminary thinking was established through the first two councils. There were two more councils (Ephesus in 431 and Chalcedon in 451). They dealt, mostly, with the nature of Christ. After all, the "co-eternal, co-equal persons" of the Godhead had been established. Well, almost. That theology was to be sealed even further.

Augustine (AD 345-430)

Augustine of Hippo is considered by many to be the "Father of Western Theology." We find two major influences in his formative trinitarian thinking. First was that of Plato. González, among others, admits he had an "open admiration for the best of pagan culture, particularly for the Platonists."[222] It was Augustine's "reading of the Neo-Platonists that clarified his understanding of God."[223] "He

---

[222] Justo González, *Christian Thought Revisited: Three Types of Theology* (Nashville: Abingdon Press: 1989), 102. By then it was often called "Neo-Platonism."

[223] Ibid., 103.

The Development of the Trinity

became a Neo-Platonist at Milan"[224] and, as Phillip Cary teaches, became "the friend of philosophy."[225] TeSelle writes: "Augustine's encounter with Platonism offered him a framework within which to understand Christian doctrine."[226] I have listed several comments to verify this foundation of Augustine. Is this not an obvious rebuke of the "hollow and deceptive philosophy" which was warned against by Paul in Colossians 2:8?

What was the philosophy that Plato believed? Plato taught that the "real" world might be understood by what we can see. "Augustine the Platonist"[227] would feel his need to put into the "seen" vocabulary the mysteries of the Godhead. Many illustrations of the trinity were used: Sun, ray, and light; fountain, stream, and flow; root, stem, and fruit; the colors of the rainbow; soul, thought, and spirit; memory, intelligence, and will. With these ideas and even the use of "person," we must understand that they are just material illustrations of the unknown.[228] As a triangle on a chalkboard illustrates the real triangle, so examples that we can see are

---

[224] Justo González, *A History of Christian Thought*, Vol. II (Nashville: Abingdon Press: 1971), 18.

[225] Phillip Cary, Lectures on CD: "Augustine: Philosopher and Saint" (Chantilly, VA: The Teaching Company, 1997), from lecture #2.

[226] TeSelle, 12.

[227] Ibid.

[228] Schaff, 677-678.

Part Three: The New Doctrine Is Mandated

illustrative of the unseen.[229]

Yet we must remember: the things of God are unseen. We must be careful in illustrations of the things of God. To whom (or what) can He be likened (Isaiah 46:5)?

Second, Augustine knew the Cappadocians' theology[230] and built upon their developing theories. Justo González writes:

> Augustine accepted Trinitarian doctrine as a matter of faith that is beyond every doubt. Therefore, his work On the Trinity is not devoted, as most of its predecessors, to offer proofs of the divinity of the Son and of the Holy Spirit, nor to prove their essential unity with the Father. Basically Augustine built upon the foundation laid by the three Cappadocians.[231]

Once again, the "fight" was over. The trinity had now developed to the point where it was a matter of acceptance by the Catholic church. All that was needed now was a "solid"

---

[229] Cary, from Lecture 8. It is hard to see Augustine's real point here, but this was his teaching.

[230] As stated earlier, Augustine's stronger dependence was on, of all three Cappadocians, Gregory of Nazianzus (TeSelle, 54).

[231] Justo González, *A History of Christian Thought*, Vol. I (Nashville: Abingdon Press: 1970), 337.

The Development of the Trinity

explanation of the trinity. From 400 to 416, Augustine wrote *De Trinitate* (On the Trinity), giving "understanding to his faith."[232] He wrote, "There is no better word than the Trinity." Here is a typical sampling from his book:

> Some are troubled in this faith when they hear that the Father is God, the Son is God, the Holy Spirit is God, and this Trinity is not three Gods but one God; and they ask how they are to conceive it.[233]

Augustine, nevertheless, was reluctant at times to use the word "persons," saying it was just the best word that mankind could find. His introduction to *De Trinitate* reveals his seeming hesitancy of dogmatism:

> If we say that we are not in the habit of thinking about subjects we are lying; on the other hand . . . we are carried away by an eagerness for investigating the truth. . . . I myself shall also derive profit by serving them with that they read, and in my eagerness to answer those who are seeking, I too, shall discover what I was seeking. Therefore, I have undertaken this work by the command and

---

[232] "Faith seeking understanding" was a theme for both Augustine and later Anselm in following Augustinian thought.

[233] Augustine, *The Trinity*, trans. Stephen McKenna (Washington, D.C., The Catholic University of America Press, 1963), 11.

Part Three: The New Doctrine Is Mandated

with the help of the Lord our God, not for the sake of speaking with authority about what I know, as to know these subjects by speaking of them with reverence.[234]

Even so, Augustine's writings cemented the thinking of the Catholic church. It was Augustine's use of the three persons being co-equal and co-eternal that had potent effect on the future of theology. Noted historian Louis Berkhof notes that it was through *On the Trinity* that "the Western conception of Trinitarian thought became solidified."[235] It had "reached its final statement."[236] What had started as conjecture had now become solidly accepted.

Augustine added another level of thought to the three persons. No one had yet developed the trinity to a degree that the doctrine of "mutual love" would evoke:

> Each person expresses the whole fullness of the divine being with its attributes and the three persons stand in a relation of mutual knowledge and love. The Father communicates his very life to the Son, and the Spirit is the bond of union and communion between the two.[237]

---

[234] Ibid., 12-13.

[235] Berkhof, 92.

[236] Ibid., 93.

[237] Schaff, 676.

The Development of the Trinity

We will have more on this after the Athanasian Creed. But any defender of monotheism should agree: The mutual love doctrine is the quintessence of tritheism.

Augustine's writings (with the exception of the doctrine of "mutual love") were used almost verbatim in the Athanasian Creed. It may be found in the next section. The exact words show the similarly to Augustine's work but this time with a warning against those who would not believe in the trinity. It would be soon mandated that only those who believed this doctrine would be saved. Let us move on to this creed.

The Athanasian Creed

The Athanasian Creed was not written by Athanasius. We know this for two reasons: First, it was actually written in a different century, sometime between 435 and 535.[238] Athanasius lived in the 300s.

Second, Athanasius was not supportive of its theories. He wrote *On the Incarnation* in his day. Not one time, though, does that document even use the words "trinity," "God the Son," or "Eternal Son" or even suggest God is three co-equal, co-eternal persons!

Athanasius fought against the Arian doctrine of the

---

[238] Ibid., 112. Kelly details his reason for these dates. While we won't find it necessary to give his reasons, most all historians agree that the creed was written somewhere around the AD 500 time, some pointing to AD 525 exactly.

Part Three: The New Doctrine Is Mandated

"second god" at the Nicean council in 325. Later trinitarian clergy named him as their "champion." He indeed was the champion, but for the incarnation of God in Christ—not for the trinitarian teaching of the Athanasian Creed.

As we have seen, it was given its final shape by the Cappadocians[239] and Augustine, especially in its categorization of persons within the Godhead. But again, it was not from the era of Athanasius. The "Quicunque"[240] is "patently post-Athanasian."[241]

Many trinitarians such as Calvin Beisner feel that the trinity "is one of the most precise statements of the essentials of the Christian faith."[242] What is the definition, then, of so important a doctrine? The Athanasian Creed, mimicking Augustine, says that:

> The Father's person is one, the Son's another, the Holy Spirit's another; but the Godhead of the Father, the Son and the Holy Spirit is one, their glory is equal, their majesty co-eternal.

If three persons who distinctively exist are co-eternal, then why is one called the Father, and the other the

---

[239] Ibid., 85.

[240] This is another name for the creed, taken from the Latin.

[241] J.N.D. Kelley, *The Athanasian Creed* (London: Adam and Charles Black, Limited, 1964), 2.

[242] Beisner, 12.

The Development of the Trinity

Son? Of course Origen had an answer, but eternal generation is neither scriptural nor understandable. The creed goes on, however. Though these three are co-eternal,

> The Father is from none, not made nor created nor begotten. The Son is from the Father alone, not made nor created but begotten. The Holy Spirit is from the Father and the Son, not made nor created nor begotten but proceeding.

The Father then stands alone, with no one creating Him. The Son is begotten. The Holy Spirit is "double proceeding."[243] Regarding these functions, there should be no problem. The question arises, though, as to when the Son was born. The Quicunque gives two answers:

> He is God from the Father's substance, begotten before time; and he is man from his mother's substance born in time.

This would give Jesus two births! Even Kelly remarks that the Athanasian Creed means Christ "has a twofold generation, before time from the Father and in time

---

[243] This "double proceeding" theory, that the Holy Spirit comes from both the Father and Son through all eternity, is called the *filoque*. It was in much debate at the Council of Toledo in 589. The *filoque* eventually was at least listed as a major reason for the East-West split in 1054.

from the Blessed Virgin."[244] Begetting is a time-based concept. Therefore, there must have been a "time when he was not." Was He the "angel of the Lord" as Tertullian suggested, a demi-God, or a Spirit that we can't label? Was He "hidden" as Gregory of Nazianzus and surmised?[245] When He was born in Bethlehem, was this His second birth? If He was really a "person" before the actual man Jesus appeared, and there were three persons in heaven, was there now a fourth "person" who was God on the earth? These are serious questions.

Why should we accept this? It is a new doctrine!

After the Athanasian Creed

The dogma of three persons that are co-equal and co-eternal became even more outrageous. The three persons became individuals who have been eternally sharing love with each other. As stated, Augustine began this teaching. This outlandish concept was built upon many times. For example, Richard of St. Victor, who was "one of the most important Trinitarian thinkers of the Middle Ages,"[246] explained that "such a sharing of love cannot exist except among less than three persons."[247] We sit at the feet of three

---

[244] Kelly, 91.

[245] Gregory of Nazianzus, Epistle 58, quoted in Pelikan, 211.

[246] McGrath, 203-204.

[247] Ibid.

The Development of the Trinity

persons and thereby understand what love is about. This is mind-boggling that the new doctrine was going this far. Francis Schaeffer, a well-known conservative Presbyterian theologian of the twentieth century, said, "there was love and communication within the Trinity."[248] More recently, a well known theologian wrote:

> The triune God is a relational community. Throughout eternity the Father, Son, and Holy Spirit have existed in a loving, interactive unity.[249]

This is tritheism at a worse stage than had ever before been attempted. This concept is not biblically supported and is nothing greater than intellectual conjecture.

Nevertheless, the trinitarian dogma became the "official teaching of the 'church.' "[250] By 383, Emperor Theodosius had threatened to punish all who would not believe in and worship the trinity.[251] Throughout the Middle Ages,

---

[248] Schaeffer is quoted in *Hymns for the Family of God* (Nashville: Paragon Associates, Inc.), 364.

[249] Glen Scorgie, *A Little Guide to Christian Spirituality: Three Dimensions of Life with God* (Grand Rapids: Zondervan, 2007), 57.

[250] Pelikan, 224.

[251] Hugh Stannus, *A History of the Origin of the Doctrine of the Trinity in the Christian Church* (London: Christian Life Publishing Company, 1882), viii.

Part Three: The New Doctrine Is Mandated

writes González, "there were few" who questioned the trinity.[252] Further, "those who did were promptly suppressed by the authorities."[253]

In the next section, we will look at the creeds themselves. What started as conjecture became the established, irrefutable doctrine of Christianity. With the final creed called the Athanasian, the trinity became the bedrock of Catholic and non-Catholic Christianity.[254] The Reformation with Luther, Calvin, and Zwingli never challenged the trinitarian beliefs. Yes, there were exceptions. Michael Servetus was burned at the stake for writing *On the Errors of the Trinity*. The Quakers refused to use the word "trinity."[255] In

---

[252] Justo González, *A Concise History of Christian Doctrine* (Nashville: Abingdon Press: 2005), 84.

[253] Ibid.

[254] As an example, The French Confession of Faith (1559) is typical of the Protestant understanding of canon and creeds. "We confess the three creeds as follows: the Apostles', the Nicene, and the Athanasian, because they are in accordance with the Word of God" (McAlister, 102-103).

[255] William Penn, for example, a well-known Quaker, was jailed about eighteen months in England, before coming to the United States, for writing and distributing *The Sandy Foundation Shaken*. While in jail, he wrote a similar pamphlet, *Innocency with her Open Face*. These writings attacked the trinitarian "foundation" of historic Christianity, providing a

The Development of the Trinity

some revivals such as the Second Awakening's Cane Ridge revival of 1801, we find men such as Barton Stone openly baptizing in the name of Jesus and refusing to use trinitarian language. He was almost put out of the Presbyterian church for it, but he told them, "This whole thing is incomprehensible." Still, the children of these revivals did not solidify their stance against the trinity. For the most part, the trinity with its peculiar notions was accepted for years as "orthodox." Whosoever would not believe in it faithfully could not be saved.[256] The new doctrine of the trinity had now been introduced, established, and finally mandated.

---

biblical understanding of the mighty God in Christ. The first document may be found on the Internet.

[256] This is the last verse of the Athanasian Creed.

The New Doctrine's Terminology: The Creeds

The council debated the doctrines. But the creeds give us something to "hold on to" historically. The development of the trinity is traced easily in the evolution of these statements.

The first creed that is recorded is the "Apostles' Creed." All historians agree that it was not written by the apostles. It was an "emerging" document and is difficult to find its exact beginning.[257] By the middle of the second century, we find it used as a general statement of faith. There is no mention of the trinity in it. The word "catholic" is meant to mean "universal," as previously mentioned.

---

[257] The only real "apostles' creed" is found in Luke's writings in the Book of Acts:

"Now when they heard this, they were pricked in their heart, and said unto Peter and to the rest of the apostles, Men and brethren, what shall we do? Then Peter said unto them, Repent, and be baptized every one of you in the name of Jesus Christ for the remission of sins, and ye shall receive the gift of the Holy Ghost. For the promise is unto you, and to your children, and to all that are afar off, even as many as the Lord our God shall call" (Acts 2:37-39).

The Development of the Trinity

The Apostles' Creed

1. I believe in God the Father, Almighty, Maker of heaven and earth:
2. And in Jesus Christ, his only begotten Son, our Lord:
3. Who was conceived by the Holy Ghost, born of the Virgin Mary:
4. Suffered under Pontius Pilate; was crucified, dead and buried: He descended into hell:
5. The third day he rose again from the dead:
6. He ascended into heaven, and sits at the right hand of God the Father Almighty:
7. From thence he shall come to judge the quick and the dead:
8. I believe in the Holy Ghost:
9. I believe in the Holy Catholic Church: the Communion of Saints:
10. The forgiveness of sins:
11. The resurrection of the body:
12. And the life everlasting. Amen.

The next two creeds are the most important. We put these together because of the importance of the development from the first to the second. The Nicene Creed is actually from the council at 325, although the 381 version is sometimes quoted as being the Nicene Creed. Notice the addition of the words "before all ages." This was not written at Nicea but added at Constantinople in 381. The words in brackets (left) were deleted, those in italics (right) added.

The New Doctrine's Terminology: The Creeds

The Nicene and Nicene-Constantinopolitan Creeds[258]

The Nicene Creed of 325	**The Constantinopolitan Creed of 281**
We believe in one God, the FATHER Almighty, Maker of all things visible and invisible.	We believe in one God, the FATHER Almighty, Maker of *heaven and earth, and of* all things visible and invisible.
And in one Lord JESUS CHRIST, the Son of God, begotten of the Father [the only-begotten; that is, of the essence of the Father, God of God], Light of Light, very God of very God, begotten, not made, being of one substance with the Father; by whom all things were made [both in heaven and on earth]; who for us men, and for our salvation,	And in one Lord JESUS CHRIST, the *only-begotten* Son of God, begotten of the Father *before all worlds*, Light of Light, very God of very God, begotten, not made, being of one substance with the Father; by whom all things were made; who for us men, and for our salvation, came down *from heaven*, and was incarnate *by the Holy Ghost of the*

---

[258] Philip Schaff, ed. *Early Church Fathers: The Translations of The Writings of the Fathers down to AD 325* [CD-Rom] Waco, Texas: Epiphany Software, 2006. The italicized words were added from the Nicene to the Constantinopolitan (or new Nicene) Creed. The bracketed words were deleted.

The Development of the Trinity

came down and was incarnate and was made man; he suffered, and the third day he rose again, ascended into heaven; from thence he shall come to judge the quick and the dead.

Virgin Mary, and was made man; *he was crucified for us under Pontius Pilate*, and suffered, *and was buried*, and the third day he rose again, *according to the Scriptures*, and ascended into heaven, and *sitteth on the right hand of the Father*; from thence he shall come *again, with glory*, to judge the quick and the dead; *whose kingdom shall have no end.*

And in the HOLY GHOST.

And in the HOLY GHOST, *the Lord and Giver of life, who proceedeth from the Father, who with the Father and the Son together is worshiped and glorified, who spake by the prophets. In one holy catholic and apostolic Church; we acknowledge one baptism for the remission of sins; we look for the resurrection of the dead, and the life of the world to come. Amen.*

The New Doctrine's Terminology: The Creeds

(But those who say: 'There was a time when he was not;' and 'He was not before he was made;' and 'He was made out of nothing,' or 'He is of another substance' or 'essence,' or 'The Son of God is created,' or 'changeable,' or 'alterable'—they are condemned by the holy catholic and apostolic Church.)

The Definition of Chalcedon

There were four major councils: Nicea in 325, Constantinople in 381, Ephesus in 431, and finally Chalcedon in 451. The first two councils' creeds are shown above. The council in Ephesus dealt with Mary, but we will not need to address the subject here. The final of the four councils, summarizing all four, produced this creed:

> We all with one voice teach that it is to be confessed that our Lord Jesus Christ is one and the same God, perfect in divinity, and perfect in humanity, true God and true human, with a rational soul and a body, of one substance with the Father in his divinity, and of one substance with us in his humanity, in every way like us, with the only exception of sin, begotten of the Father before all

The Development of the Trinity

times in his divinity, and also begotten in the latter days, in his humanity, of Mary the virgin bearer of God.[259]

Now, Jesus surely has two births: sometime in eternity and also at Bethlehem. This is more outrageous than the Constantinopolitan Creed.

As stated, clearly the Athanasian Creed is wrongly named. However, this creed is used to seal the Catholic and later Protestants' formula of belief. The reader (the Christian) is asked to believe something that is not comprehensible, and if he or she cannot, he cannot be saved. Why the Protestant movement did not fully reject this Catholic doctrine is left to our own conjecture. But maybe we have "come to the kingdom for such a time as this." We must be willing to re-examine what the "fathers" gave us, to see if it be truth or tradition. At any rate, here is the creed:

The Athanasian Creed[260]

1. Whosoever will be saved, before all things it is necessary that he hold the catholic faith;
2. Which faith except every one do keep whole and undefiled, without doubt he shall perish everlastingly.

---

[259] Justo González, *The Story of Christianity*, Vol. I. (Peabody, Mass: Prince Press, 2001), 257.

[260] Ibid., Schaff.

The New Doctrine's Terminology: The Creeds

3. And the catholic faith is this: That we worship one God in Trinity, and Trinity in Unity;
4. Neither confounding the persons nor dividing the substance.
5. For there is one person of the Father, another of the Son, and another of the Holy Spirit.
6. But the Godhead of the Father, of the Son, and of the Holy Spirit is all one, the glory equal, the majesty coeternal.
7. Such as the Father is, such is the Son, and such is the Holy Spirit.
8. The Father uncreated, the Son uncreated, and the Holy Spirit uncreated.
9. The Father incomprehensible, the Son incomprehensible, and the Holy Spirit incomprehensible.
10. The Father eternal, the Son eternal, and the Holy Spirit eternal.
11. And yet they are not three eternals but one eternal.
12. As also there are not three uncreated nor three incomprehensible, but one uncreated and one incomprehensible.
13. So likewise the Father is almighty, the Son almighty, and the Holy Spirit almighty.
14. And yet they are not three almighties, but one almighty.
15. So the Father is God, the Son is God, and the Holy Spirit is God;
16. And yet they are not three Gods, but one God.
17. So likewise the Father is Lord, the Son Lord, and the Holy Spirit Lord;

The Development of the Trinity

18. And yet they are not three Lords but one Lord.
19. For like as we are compelled by the Christian verity to acknowledge every Person by himself to be God and Lord;
20. So are we forbidden by the catholic religion to say; There are three Gods or three Lords.
21. The Father is made of none, neither created nor begotten.
22. The Son is of the Father alone; not made nor created, but begotten.
23. The Holy Spirit is of the Father and of the Son; neither made, nor created, nor begotten, but proceeding.
24. So there is one Father, not three Fathers; one Son, not three Sons; one Holy Spirit, not three Holy Spirits.
25. And in this Trinity none is afore or after another; none is greater or less than another.
26. But the whole three persons are coeternal, and coequal.
27. So that in all things, as aforesaid, the Unity in Trinity and the Trinity in Unity is to be worshipped.
28. He therefore that will be saved must thus think of the Trinity.
29. Furthermore it is necessary to everlasting salvation that he also believe rightly the incarnation of our Lord Jesus Christ.
30. For the right faith is that we believe and confess that our Lord Jesus Christ, the Son of God, is God and man.

The New Doctrine's Terminology: The Creeds

31. God of the substance of the Father, begotten before the worlds; and man of substance of His mother, born in the world.
32. Perfect God and perfect man, of a reasonable soul and human flesh subsisting.
33. Equal to the Father as touching His Godhead, and inferior to the Father as touching His manhood.
34. Who, although He is God and man, yet He is not two, but one Christ.
35. One, not by conversion of the Godhead into flesh, but by taking of that manhood into God.
36. One altogether, not by confusion of substance, but by unity of person.
37. For as the reasonable soul and flesh is one man, so God and man is one Christ;
38. Who suffered for our salvation, descended into hell, rose again the third day from the dead;
39. He ascended into heaven, He sits on the right hand of the Father, God, Almighty;
40. From thence He shall come to judge the quick and the dead.
41. At whose coming all men shall rise again with their bodies;
42. and shall give account of their own works.
43. And they that have done good shall go into life everlasting and they that have done evil into everlasting fire.
44. This is the catholic faith, which except a man believe faithfully he cannot be saved.

Non-biblical Words Used in Church History

The "new doctrine" of the trinity used newly invented words. The following research is of terminological words that are not in the Bible. They can be found so common in Christendom that we would assume them to be in the Scriptures. But great caution and even suspicion should be employed in their usage if we want to be genuinely theologically "orthodox." The words in question are "God the Son," "God the Holy Spirit" (or Ghost), "Eternal Son," "co-equal," and "co-eternal." Here we note the "first mention" of these phrases in the history of the church.[261]

God the Son

This is found in Athenagkorus's *A Plea for the Christians*, chapter ten: "The Christians Worship the Father,

---

[261] All research was done by electronic searches from Philip Schaff, ed. *Early Church Fathers: The Translations of The Writings of the Fathers down to AD 325* [CD-Rom] Waco, Texas: Epiphany Software, 2006. Schaff is indisputedly conclusive for this purpose.

The Development of the Trinity

Son, and Holy Ghost." The year was AD 177. Not too long after that, we find the phrase in Clement of Alexandria. He mentions the "Blood of God the Son" in *The Salvation of the Rich Man*. Later references were made by Tertullian, Novatian (in arguments against the modalists), and others.

God the Holy Spirit

There is not a mention of this term (or "God the Holy Ghost") in the early patristic era. In the early 400s, Augustine, in his *On the Holy Trinity* (Book 15, Chapter 17,"How the Holy Spirit is Called, Love, and Whether He alone is so Called…"), writes:

> But they have said, "God is love," so that it is uncertain and remains to be inquired whether God the Father is love, or God the Son, or God the Holy Ghost, or the Trinity itself which is God.

Eternal Son

Clement of Alexandria (c. 150–215) first used this term in the *Exhortation to the Heathen*, chapter 12. Later this phrase was in the "Liturgy of the Blessed Apostles," by St. Adaeus and St. Maris, "Teachers of the Easterns":

> Holy art Thou, O God our Father, truly the only one, of whom the whole family in heaven and hearth is named. Holy art Thou, Eternal Son, through whom all things were made. Holy art

Thou, Holy, Eternal Spirit, through whom all things are sanctified.

Further, we find frequent use of the term in Augustine's *On the Holy Trinity*. Also, in his *Lectures on the Gospel According to St. John* (Tractate 21), Augustine wrote:

> For He is the Son equal to the Father, the eternal Son with the Father, and co-eternal with the Father, but we became sons through the Son, adopted through the Only-begotten.

Co-equal

We find no use of the term "co-equal" in the earlier patristic documents, even though the Cappadocians and the Council of Constantinople propagated the theology with different words. In a short time later, though, Augustine used the term in his book *On the Holy Trinity*:

> The Father hath begotten the Son, and so He who is the Father is not the Son; and the Son is begotten by the Father, and so He who is the Son is not the Father; and the Holy Spirit is neither the Father nor the Son, but only the Spirit of the Father and of the Son, Himself also co-equal with the Father and the Son, and pertaining to the unity of the Trinity.[262]

---

[262] Book 1, Chapter 4.

The Development of the Trinity

Co-eternal

We first find a mention of this in *The Extant Works and Fragments of Hippolytus* (AD 170-236), not with the typical later trinitarian definition of the Son,[263] but nonetheless used:

> Thou Friend of man, when saw we Thee sick or in prison, and came unto Thee? Thou art the ever-living One. Thou art without beginning, like the Father, and co-eternal with the Spirit. Thou art He who made all things out of nothing. Thou art the prince of the angels. Thou art He at whom the depths tremble. Thou art He who is covered with light as with a garment. Thou art He who made us, and fashioned us of earth. Thou art He who formed things invisible. From Thy presence the whole earth fleeth away.

Later this term and the others were used much in Augustine's writings, such as *On the Trinity*. Here is a sample from another of his writings, *Instructing the Unlearned*:

> For this same Christ, the only-begotten Son of God, the Word of the Father, equal and co-eternal with the Father, by whom all things were made,

---

[263] It appears as if the writer was referring to Jesus as the creator rather than the "second person," although he also called Jesus "like" the Father.

Non-biblical Words Used in Church History

was Himself also made man for our sakes, in order that of the whole Church, as of His whole body, He might be the Head.[264]

It is amazing that these labels were absent not only from the Scriptures but also from the first one hundred years of the church's history. Why should we look upon them today as orthodox?

---

[264] Chapter 19.

Summary

The following pages will put this study into an easy "nutshell." We begin the review of the development of the trinity with the distinguished patristics scholar David Wright:

> The doctrine of the Trinity is one of the most distinctive and fundamental tenets of the Christian faith. It was during the patristic centuries that the church's Trinitarian faith assumed the shape it has largely retained throughout its history.[265]

The Apologists and the Logos

The Greek Apologists taught that God was not capable of emotion and interaction. Thus, He had created the Logos that was separate from him. "God, being spaceless and infinite, was in need of the Logos as a middle being to bridge the gap and chasm between him and the world."[266]

---

[265] David Wright, "Trinity," *Encyclopedia of Early Christianity*, ed. Everett Ferguson (New York: Garland Publishers, 1997), 1142. Wright taught at Edinburgh University for more than forty years.

[266] Heick, *A History of Christian Thought*, Vol. I (Philadelphia: Fortress Press, 1965), 59.

The Development of the Trinity

Later, the Christian Apologists identified Christ as the pre-existent Logos. "The concept of the pre-existent Christ is the most significant factor in the development [of the trinity]."[267]

Justin Martyr (AD 100–165)

"We can indisputably learn that God conversed with someone who was numerically distinct from Himself, and also a rational Being."[268] (Genesis 1:26, "Let us create....")

Tertullian (AD 160–220)

"Tertullian takes his starting point in the doctrine of the Logos, but develops it in a way that became historically significant. The Logos is . . . an independent Person. . . . He enlarged the doctrine of the Logos into the doctrine of the Trinity."[269]

---

[267] Loofs, *Nestoriana: Die Fragmente des Destorius*. (Halle, 1905), 314-315. Quoted by Pelikan, 189.

[268] Justin, *Second Apology*, Ch. 62, Schaff, *Early Church Fathers*.

[269] Louis Berkhof, *The History of Christian Doctrines* (Carlisle, Penn.: The Banner of Truth, 1937), 65.

Summary

Origen (AD 185–254)

If the Son is a separate person who was pre-existent yet is begotten by the Father, when did the Father beget Him? Origen answers: "The Father . . . is always begetting Him."[270] This became known as "eternal generation."

The Councils of Nicea (AD 325) and Constantinople (AD 381)

The pre-Bethlehem begetting of the Son was not adopted into the first creed but was added into the modified creed in 381:

> And we believe in one Lord Jesus Christ . . . begotten of the Father *before all worlds*, Light of Light, very God of very God, begotten, not made, being of one substance with the Father.

Note added words to the Nicene Creed—shown in italics.

The Definition of Chalcedon (AD 451)

Jesus was begotten twice: Before all ages, and also in the womb of Mary.

---

[270] Otto Heick, *A History of Christian Thought*, Vol. I (Philadelphia: Fortress Press, 1965), 53.

The Development of the Trinity

Augustine of Hippo (AD 345–430)

Augustine expounded the theology of the trinity in his book, *On the Trinity*:

> The Father is God, the Son is God, the Holy Spirit is God, and this Trinity is not three Gods but one God.[271]

The Athanasian Creed (c. AD 525)

Augustine's writings were used as a foundation for the next major creed. This "statement of faith" was named for Athanasius, who lived two centuries earlier.[272] It became the basis of the Catholic and most Protestant churches. "Three separate, co-equal, co-eternal persons" would become part of the creedal statements of major churches.

> "The Father's person is one, the Son's another, the Holy Spirit's another; but the Godhead of the

---

[271] Augustine, *The Trinity*, trans. Stephen McKenna (Washington, D.C., The Catholic University of America Press, 1963), 11.

[272] There was not one mention of the word "Trinity" in Athanasius' main work, *On the Incarnation*. Athanasius was called the "champion" of Nicea but surely did not develop the co-equal, co-eternal status of the persons. His mission was against the errors of Arius.

Summary

Father, the Son and the Holy Spirit is one, their glory is equal, their majesty co-eternal."

Final Stages

Statements such as the following began to appear:

"Such a sharing of love cannot exist except among less than three persons."[273]

"The triune God is a relational community. Throughout eternity the Father, Son, and Holy Spirit have existed in a loving, interactive unity."[274]

---

[273] Richard of St. Victor, quoted by McGrath, 267.

[274] Glen Scorgie, *A Little Guide to Christian Spirituality: Three Dimensions of Life with God* (Grand Rapids: Zondervan, 2007), 57.

Reflections

It appears, in retrospect of the developing dogma of the trinity, that Paul was prophetically warning the Colossians: "See to it that no one takes you captive through hollow and deceptive philosophy, which depends on human tradition and the basic principles of this world rather than on Christ" (Colossians 2:8, NIV). The Godhead issue was offered simply in the next verse: "For in Christ all the fullness of the Deity lives in bodily form." God was in Christ, reconciling the world to Himself (II Corinthians 5:19). Paul did not seem to explain the issues beyond this point. McGrath says there is always a "growing trend to crystallize central defining Christian insights into short formulas for pedagogic and defensive purposes."[275] In other words, the Godhead was turned into philosophical formulas —exactly what Paul warned against.

    Millard J. Erickson wrote a theological book that is used at many seminaries. In his chapter on the trinity, he remarks: "In the final analysis, the Trinity is incomprehensible. We cannot fully understand the mystery of the Trinity."[276] "In practice," he adds, "even orthodox Christians

---

[275] McGrath, 175.

[276] Millard J. Erickson, *Christian Theology*, Second Edition (Grand Rapids: Baker Academic, 1998), 363.

The Development of the Trinity

have difficulty clinging simultaneously to the several components of the doctrine."[277] I agree. The trinity is seldom accepted equally across the board. Yet paradoxically it is used as a screening of orthodoxy for Christians, ministers, Bible schools' potential students, and so on.[278] Curiously, Erickson begins his finish of this chapter on the trinity with a different tone:

> The doctrine of the Trinity is a crucial ingredient of our faith, . . . It is appropriate to direct prayers of thanks and petitions to each of the members of the Trinity, as well as to all of them collectively.[279]

There is no Scripture that supports this. If each "person" must receive his equal praise, then they are real people with jealousy between them.

Erickson's last word on the issue is a quote of "someone" who observes the paradox of trying to understand the trinity:

> Try to explain it, and you'll lose your mind;
> But try to deny it and you'll lose your soul.[280]

---

[277] Ibid., 365.

[278] This was not a screen used by Bethel for potential students. I understand it was a requirement that was lifted several years ago.

[279] Erickson, 367.

[280] Ibid.

Reflections

While that has a touch of humor, it does not hold water. The Athanasian Creed asks us to know that the trinity is incomprehensible, yet not believing it will supposedly damn our souls. How can we be asked to believe something that we cannot understand, and yet if we do not believe it we will be lost?[281]

It stands as a fact of history that early disciples obeyed Matthew 28:19 and Luke 24:47 by baptizing in the name of Jesus.[282] As the trinitarian mode came into

---

[281] Please see the last verse of the Athanasian Creed. It is in the chapter about the major creeds.

[282] Some, as Basil, suggested that baptism in the name of Jesus was only an "abbreviated reference to the same thing." (Bernard, ibid.) I find that theory insufficient. Also, there are theories that Matthew 28:19 was originally "in my name" and was changed. Eusebius, the first church historian, quoted Matthew in the shorter formula before the Nicene council. For this mention and a detailed argument that "in the name of the Father, and of the Son, and of the Holy Ghost" was interpolated by subsequent trinitarian generations, see G. R. Beasley-Murray, *Baptism in the New Testament* (London: MacMillan & Co, Ltd; New York: St. Martin's Press, Inc. 1962), 77-81. Agreeing with this possibility is David Reed, *In Jesus' Name* (Blandford Forum, Ddorset DT11 1AQ, UK) 243. If this is so, we would have a further explanation of why baptism in the name of Jesus was the only baptism until about AD 130. Of course, this whole theory is not "etched in stone" and raises other controversial questions.

The Development of the Trinity

existence, so did the theology of the trinity.

The word "trinity" is not found in the Scripture, but that in itself should not exclude its use. Although a certain theological word is not found in the Scriptures, we still may be inclined to use it. (And that use should be with great caution; *homoousios* was surely no success!) To be a valid theological term, though, the word used must have a biblical, revelatory meaning.

The chief problematic definition of the word "trinity," I submit, is that it reflects the Platonically inspired pre-existence theory of the Logos, which became the Christ. If Christ pre-existed, how? Ancient pre-Christian Greek philosophy would present him as a pre-existent, co-existent soul. When Christianity mixed this, He was a pre-existent deity separate—even "numerically distinct" from God. If Christ were pre-existent and co-equal and co-eternal as a separate deity in heaven as the Son before his nativity, our basic monotheistic foundation of "one God" (as in Deuteronomy 6:4) would be destroyed.

González, looking at the whole patristic era and its definitions, summarizes:

> A general evaluation of the development of Christian thought up to the time of the Council of Chalcedon should affirm that the development involves without any doubt a profound Hellenization of Christianity. That Hellenization has to do not only with matters of form or vocabulary, but also with the very understanding of the nature of Christianity, and it therefore created problems that

Reflections

ideally could have been avoided by following other avenues of philosophical interpretation.[283]

The question in many minds is: What about the word "persons"? Since this is such an important part of the definition and history of the trinity, what should be meant by this terminology? Richardson answers this question:

> It depends upon the view which we take of the meaning of the word "person." **Those who formulated the Church's doctrine of the Trinity did not mean by "person" what we mean by it today.** . . . It is often assumed that the Christian doctrine of the Trinity commits us to belief in the Godhead as consisting of three separate personalities, and certainly many churchmen thus interpret the doctrine today. Such an interpretation is called the "social doctrine" of the Trinity, because the Godhead is thus held to be a society of persons. **It is hard to see how any formulation of this view can logically avoid the charge of Tritheism.**[284]

In bold are Richardson's "bold" remarks! Many have asked the question, "What is the difference between the trinitarian position of "God in three persons, blessed

---

[283] González, 394.

[284] Richardson, 60.

The Development of the Trinity

Trinity"[285] and the Oneness position of "One God in three offices"? What is wrong with the word "persons"? My answer is this: "Persons" came to mean three individuals who can talk to each other. These persons are defined as co-equal and co-eternal. This means that Jesus was pre-existent in His Deity before His birth, being both eternal and equal. Then the Holy Spirit becomes (by the second council in AD 381) another person co-equal to the others and can converse with them. This is not biblical monotheism, but as Richardson says, it is tritheism.

If any developer of the trinitarian doctrine should be accurately charged with tritheism, it would be Augustine. His summary of the trinity being the "eternal Father loving the eternal Son through the eternal Spirit" is nothing less than intellectual conjecture. When it comes to the word "persons," however, even he stated, "We say three persons, not in order to express it, but in order not to be silent."[286]

(It should be noted that the words "God in three persons" were not used by the church "fathers" until Augustine. We find them used once by Augustine in *On the Trinity* [Book 12, Ch. 5]. This set of words was most likely made famous by the hymn "Holy, Holy, Holy," written by Reginald Heber in 1826, and with music added by John

---

[285] This is the name of the well-known song first called "Nicea." See below.

[286] Heick, 166.

Reflections

Dykes in 1861.[287])

Kelly notices that "Augustine . . . is clearly unhappy about the term"[288] because of its ambiguity. Gregory Boyd, after taking notice of Augustine's statement, says,

> There is simply no better term available. . . . It is for this reason that I deem it expedient to put the word "person" in quotes, reminding the reader that we are using the word in a unique, non-literal sense.[289]

Would quotes around the word "persons" work? What reader would not still think of the "persons" that were developed through the ages—co-equal and co-eternal? The new doctrine has been too developed to go back again.

Philosophy should never have been mixed with divine revelation. Jesus told Peter that "flesh and blood hath

---

[287] A further study could help substantiate this premise, but it is interesting that "God in three persons" is non-existent in the first three centuries of the church. (Research was done electronically with *Early Church Fathers*.) In the 1916 watershed rejection of Oneness by the Assemblies of God in its infant stage, the words were sung almost as sacredly as if they were from the Scriptures.

[288] Kelly, *Doctrines*, 274.

[289] Boyd, 163. Boyd also remarks that Augustine was "uncomfortable" with the word "trinity" (ibid., 173).

The Development of the Trinity

not revealed" the Christ's identity (Matthew 16:17). Paul wrote that the gospel he preached was "not after man" (Galatians 1:11). The God of heaven that was eternal stepped into time and was "manifest in the flesh" (I Timothy 3:16).[290] That is who Jesus is. This is the mystery of godliness: He became like one of us, to make us the sons (and daughters) of God. But it was not a pre-existent second god who did this: it was God.

So that there is no misunderstanding: No one is claiming all perfect knowledge. Even Frank Ewart, the preacher who spearheaded the Oneness movement in 1913 and 1914, wrote these words:

> Every unit of Christendom has the apparent characteristic of turning the life stream of Calvary into a sectarian channel. They announce, by the introduction of particular and distinctive laws and rules regarding fellowship, their belief that life and power depend on a correct system of doctrine.

---

[290] The KJV reading of I Timothy 3:16 reads "God" was manifest. I am aware that some of the new versions, based upon different manuscripts, say "He" or something similar. The best refutation that I have read on this is from Adam Clarke's commentary. He wrote, "The enemies of the Deity of Christ have been at as much pains to destroy the evidence afforded by the common reading in support of this doctrine." He went on to explain the errors of the word "He" rather than the word "God" who was manifested in the flesh.

Reflections

This is not necessarily so at all. On the other hand, the more intricate doctrine you have the more divided you really are. They had no doctrine at Pentecost, but they had such a unity as the world has never seen since.

Do not misunderstand me . . . a body of doctrine is bound to grow up around Him. We cannot do without doctrine. But let it be continually held in the white light of His Person, and be maintained under the constant corrective of his Holy Life. Let us remind ourselves that no creed can give life; no doctrinal truth, however ennobling, can save a human soul from death. They must be saved by a Person, only a Person, and by One Person.[291]

Frank Ewart was not saying that doctrine is not important. Neither am I.[292] But the point is this: We need to let the Spirit of God teach, and we need to stay only with Bible doctrine. So I am not claiming that wisdom died with me or "us" in our Oneness camp. But I am claiming that intellectual conjecture took the place of revelation. This was

---

[291] Frank Ewart, *The Name and the Book* (Hazelwood, Mo: Word Aflame Press, 1986 [Original copyright 1936]), 105-106.

[292] My agreement with Ewart concurs with Howard Goss's comment in the 1910s: "We cannot reduce Christ to a formula." We must love Jesus first, and then His doctrine must be upheld. Not vice versa.

The Development of the Trinity

done in the era of church councils, under the influence of Greek philosophy.

We will briefly bring this up to date. In 1913, a "new movement" began. Great revival had been sweeping the United States for about seven years. At a camp meeting near Los Angeles, an unknown Canadian evangelist[293] was asked to conduct the baptismal service. He announced that baptism in the Scriptures was always done in the name of Jesus, not in the historically subsequent use of the "name of the Father, and of the Son. . . ." This was the "shot that had been heard around the world," according to the Frank Ewart. It was a full year before Ewart publicly baptized his assistant in the name of Jesus. His assistant in turn baptized Garfield Haywood. And we have our history.

The movement of Pentecostals baptizing in the name of Jesus was called the "New Issue." This is a curious name. Was it really new? After all, baptism in Jesus' name was hardly something "new" that began in the twentieth century. Its beginnings may be found in the first century—in the Book of Acts! In fact, a "new issue" began in the late second century. The "new issue" began with Martyr, Tertullian, Origen, and Augustine. The "new issue" was a "new doctrine." That new doctrine is the trinity. Hopefully, my newfound friend[294] will refuse to believe its teaching.

---

[293] Robert McAlister.

[294] Please see the Preface!

Annotated Bibliography

Augustine. *The Trinity.* Translated by Stephen McKenna. Washington, D.C., The Catholic University of America Press, 1963. This is *the* theological book of the fifth century that solidified the co-equal, co-existent thoughts of the ensuing ages.

Beasley-Murray, G. R. *Baptism in the New Testament.* London: MacMillan & Co, Ltd; New York: St. Martin's Press, Inc. 1962. This author is quite thorough. Baptism is covered not only from the viewpoint of Acts but also from church history.

Beisner, E. Calvin. *God in Three Persons.* Wheaton: Tyndale House Publishers, 1984. This book is well known and often used as a defense of trinitarianism.

Bercot, David, editor. *A Dictionary of Early Christian Beliefs: A Reference Guide to More Than 700 Topics Discussed by the Early Church Fathers.* Peabody, Mass: Hendrickson Publishers, 1998. These 700 topics are covered in more than 700 pages of quotes from early Christian writers. Best of all, primary sources are quoted.

Berkhof, Louis. *The History of Christian Doctrines.* Carlisle, Penn.: The Banner of Truth, 1937. The

The Development of the Trinity

author is a respected theological historian.

Bernard, David. *A History of Christian Doctrine, The Post-Apostolic Age to the Middle Ages, AD 100-1500*, Vol. I. Hazelwood, Mo.: Word Aflame Press, 1995. It is written from the viewpoint of an Oneness Pentecostal. Bernard is the most prolific historian representing the United Pentecostal Church.

_____. *The Trinitarian Controversy in the Fourth Century*. Hazelwood, Mo.: Word Aflame Press, 1993. This is an excellent source.

_____. *Oneness and Trinity, AD 100-300: The Doctrine of God in Ancient Writings*. Hazelwood, Mo.: Word Aflame Press, 1991. This also is excellent reading on the subject. These two books are a "must read" on the topic of the development of the trinity.

Boyd, Gregory. *Oneness Pentecostals & the Trinity*. Grand Rapids: Baker Book House, 1992. Boyd, once with UPC, criticizes the Oneness movement, UPC, and Bernard. His book has "made the rounds" and should be read.

Cary, Phillip. Lectures on CD: "Augustine: Philosopher and Saint." Chantilly, VA: The Teaching Company, 1997. Cary is a lecturer and seminary professor. This CD is easy to listen to and explains Augustine's theologies.

Annotated Bibliography

Carroll, Michael. *Trinitas: A Theological Encyclopedia of the Holy Trinity.* (Wilmington, Del: M. Glazier, 1987). Carroll, a Roman Catholic writer, offers a great reference tool for the subject.

Erickson, Millard J. *Christian Theology*, Second Edition. Grand Rapids: Baker Academic, 1998. (See chapter 16: "God's Three-in-Oneness: The Trinity," 346-367.) This is a standard theological source for seminary students. Because of that, this chapter should be helpful to understand modern definitions of the trinity.

Ferm, Vergilius. *A History of Philosophical Systems.* New York: The Philosophical Library, 1950. This is great reading for someone interested in Socrates, Plato, Aristotle, Philo, etc., and how they influenced the Christian era.

González, Justo L. *A History of Christian Thought.* Nashville: Abingdon Press: 1970-1971. This book follows trends throughout the centuries. This author is one of the best in church history, and his books are easy to read. He is probably also the most prolific in the field. Also recommended are *A Concise History of Christian Doctrine* and *Christian Thought Revisited*, both published by Abingdon.

_____. *The Story of Christianity*, Peabody, Massachusetts: Prince Press, 1984. This is the main textbook used at many Bible schools and post-graduate schools for courses in church history. Particularly helpful are chapters 17, 19, and 20, which deal with the development of trinitarian theology.

Grenz, Stanley J., David Guetzki, and Cherith Fee Nordling. *Pocket Dictionary of Theological Terms*. Downers Grove, Ill.: InterVarsity Press. 1999. Traditional definitions are cited.

Grillmeier, Aloys. *Christ in the Christian Tradition*, Vol. I. New York: Sheed and Ward, 1964. This is a very detailed story early history of Christology from AD 100 to 451.

Harnack, Adolph. *History of Dogma*, Vol. II, IV, trans. Neil Buchanan. New York: Dover Publications, 1961. This author is known for his opinion of the Hellenization of Christianity. He is respected by some and criticized by others.

Heick, Otto W. *A History of Christian Thought*, Vol. I. Philadelphia: Fortress Press, 1965. This author is one of the best and most respected. Moderate reading. This source was probably the most quoted in this search.

Kelly, J.N.D. *Early Christian Creeds*. New York: David McKay Company, Inc., 1960. Kelly is one of the

Annotated Bibliography

most respected historians. Sometimes his writing is difficult to read, but it is well worth the effort.

_____. *Early Christian Doctrines*. London: Adam and Charles Black, 1958. This is one of Kelly's most well-read books.

_____. *The Athanasian Creed*. London: Adam and Charles Black, Limited, 1964. Kelly does a great job with the historical and theological implications of this important creed.

McCready, Douglass. "He Came Down from Heaven: The Pre-existence of Christ Revisited." *Journal of the Evangelical Theological Society* 40/3 September 1997, 419-432. The author revisits the issue.

McGrath, Alister. *The Christian Theology Reader*. Second Edition. Malden, Ma: Blackwell Publishing, 2001. (Chapter 3: The Theology of God: 170-44) McGrath is the editor of this book on primary sources. His own comments are included. This book is typically used in Bible Schools and seminaries. The book contains a great supply of primary sources.

McKim, Donald K. *Theological Turning Points; Major Issues in Christian Thought*. Atlanta: John Knox Press, 1988. McKim's book is a summary of historical watersheds. The reader should find his writings easy to comprehend.

The Development of the Trinity

Meredith, Anthony. *The Cappodocians*. Crestwood, New York: St. Vladimer's Seminary Press, 2000. This is probably the most complete book on the three Cappadocians.

Olson, Roger E, and Adam C. English. *Pocket History of Theology*. Downers Grove, Ill.: InterVarsity Press, 2005. It is often used at seminaries and Bible Schools.

Payne, Robert, "A Hammer Struck at Heresy Christian History," *Christian History*, Issue 51. This article details the controversies of the Nicean council. Many other very helpful articles are also found in other articles of Issue 51 ("Heresy in the Church), as well as in Issue 85 ("The Council of Nicaea: Debating Jesus' Divinity"). The entire set of issues may be obtained at www.ChristianHistory.net.

Pelikan, Jaroslav. *The Christian Tradition; A History of the Development of Doctrine; Vol. I: The Emergence of the Catholic Tradition (100-600)*. Chicago: University of Chicago Press, 1971. He is absolutely one of the most respected historians, along with Heick and González.

Richardson, Alan. *Creeds in the Making: A Short Introduction to the History of Christian Doctrine*. Great Britain, Macmillan Company, 1935. This is a readable summary of the development of important

Annotated Bibliography

doctrines, including the trinity.

Schaff, Philip. *History of the Christian Church, Vol. III: Nicene and Post-Nicene Christianity: From Constantine the Great to Gregory the Great, AD 311-300*. Grand Rapids: Eerdmans Publishing Company, 1910. Schaff's work (as is Kelly's) is a well-respected reference for primary sources.

_____, editor, *Early Church Fathers*. CD-ROM. Waco, Texas: Epiphany Software, 2006. Originally this was a three-volume series of 18,000 pages. The disk form provides opportunities to do electronic searches of all known post-apostolic writers into the ninth century. It must work as an addition to *Word Search*, also available from Epiphany. I strongly recommend both disks.

Stannus, Hugh. *A History of the Origin of the Doctrine of the Trinity in the Christian Church*. London: Christian Life Publishing Company, 1882. This author is not well known in scholastic circles but points to some interesting issues.

TeSelle, Eugene. *Augustine*. Nashville: Abingdon Press, 2006. This is an easy-to-read book on all the theories of Augustine.

Wand, J.W.C. *The Four Councils*. Great Britain, Faith Press, Ltd., 1951. This author covers thoroughly the councils of 325 (Nicea), 381 (Constantinople), 431 (Ephesus), and 451 (Chalcedon). It is a bit wordy but very complete.

Wright, David, "Trinity," *Encyclopedia of Early Christianity*. Edited by Everett Ferguson. New York: Garland Publishers, 1997. A fairly easy-to-read summary of the development of the trinity.

One last note: Thank you for reading! Feel free to comment or to contact me for seminars in this or related subjects.
Email: glen-davidson@bethel.edu

To order more books, please contact:
pentecostalpublishing.com